BECOMING GOLD

THE POIGNANT STORY OF MY JOURNEY FROM TRAUMA TO TRIUMPH

DAPO LIPEDE

BECOMING GOLD

The Poignant Story Of My Journey
From Trauma To Triumph

Paperback ISBN: 978-1-965593-77-6

Published by Cornerstone Publishing

A Division of Cornerstone Creativity Group LLC
Info@thecornerstonepublishers.com
www.thecornerstonepublishers.com

Author's Contact

To book the author to speak at your next event or to order bulk copies of this book, please, use the information below:

dapolipede@gmail.com

Printed in the United States of America.

DEDICATION

This book is dedicated to:

To everyone who entered marriage with high hopes but was silenced, bruised, and broken by the very ones they loved.

To everyone who walked through the fire of marital abuse and emerged carrying wisdom, not ashes.

To everyone who survived what was meant to break them, silence them, or steal their identity.

To everyone who cried in secret, prayed in the dark, and still chose to rise when rising felt impossible.

To everyone who kept breathing when the weight was unbearable, who kept believing when hope felt distant, and who kept moving even when strength was gone.

May these pages speak life to the places that still tremble, courage to the places that still question, and truth to the places that are still healing.

To everyone who survived what should have broken them, this book is for you. You are seen. You are valued. And you are God's mosaic masterpiece in the making.

CONTENTS

ACKNOWLEDGMENTS

First and foremost, I give all the glory to God, who chose the covenant of life over the covenant of marriage in my story. Thank You, Lord, for preserving my life and giving me the grace to live, heal, and share this testimony.

To my biological children, my sisters, and my dear brother, thank you for your unwavering love and support throughout my trauma and healing journey. I truly could not have made it without you. I am deeply grateful for each of you.

To my friends, Bola, Funke O., Toky, Yinka S., Pastor Chris, and many others too numerous to mention, thank you for standing with me in some of the darkest moments of my life, when everything seemed uncertain and overwhelming. Your presence meant more than words can express.

A special thank you to my dear friend, Olufunke Adeleye, for walking closely with me in the difficult season after I made the courageous decision to walk away from abuse. Your daily calls brought comfort, strength, and healing.

To AFL, thank you for the constant reminder that my trauma was not the end of my assignment. My story is still unfolding, and hope is still alive.

And to my adopted children, I cannot leave you out. Thank you for loving me through it all. I love you deeply.

INTRODUCTION

The Story of Wura- A Tale of Suppression and Oppression

"The ultimate tragedy is not the oppression and cruelty by the bad people, but the silence over that by the good people." - Martin Luther King, Jr.

Welcome to this narrative. Let me begin by explaining why I chose *"Becoming Gold"* for the title of the book you hold in your hands. The scripture in 2 Timothy 2:20 says, *"But in a great house there are not only vessels of gold and silver, but also of wood and clay, some for honor and some for dishonor."*

My name is *Wura*, and I was born by grace to be a *vessel of gold* in the house of God. Wura is the Yorúbá word for gold, and among the Yorúbá, the word gold itself assumes the literal meaning of *precious*. My maternal grandmother gave me the name Wura to signify just how precious I was to her—her first granddaughter. Though I was born to be a vessel of gold, I still needed refinement. Gold must be refined in fire for it to become truly valuable. To refine gold is to subject it to the process of removing impurities from its raw form and produce a purer form of the precious metal. This is typically done to improve the metal's quality and increase its value.

I am *gold (Wura)*. My marriage was a *furnace*, and through this marital journey, I have been intensely *refined*. Through the refining fire, I can now appreciate God's grace in my life. I am ready to be the vessel of gold I was created to be. My traumatic marital journey was one of becoming gold, and this informed the choice of *Becoming Gold* as the title of this book.

The story of Wura is not just my story. It is the story of countless women across the globe who have no *voice* and are too frightened to speak out and expose their spouses for the abusers they are. It is very sad that spousal abuse has become an epidemic and has found a troubling place within the Body of Christ, the church of Jesus Christ. To underscore just how much of an epidemic spousal abuse has become, countless female victims of marital abuse experience unrelenting verbal intimidation, severe emotional condescension, and even physical assault. The Centers for Disease Control and Prevention (CDC) reports that *"Four million women per year are victims of violence perpetrated, in many cases, by men who vowed to love, honor, and cherish them, and approximately 1,200 women will be killed every year by those same men."* Many of these women suffer from physical and psychological trauma, with damaging and long-lasting health outcomes, while a greater number suffer from short-term and long-lasting emotional, physical, and financial consequences. It is documented that women who suffer abuse in marriage are vulnerable to developing deep-seated psychological fear and anxiety, PTSD, insomnia, depressed mood, substance use and abuse, and many other serious health issues.

Indeed, too many women have been broken, bruised, and damaged by the men they fell in love with and eventually married. Some of these women have lost their lives to domestic violence, while others have descended into mental breakdowns because of the trauma they endured in their marriages. What, unfortunately, gives cause for genuine concern is that many such women are unaware that they are being subjected to abuse. Of far graver concern is the fact that when they do recognize abuse for what it is and seek help in the house of God, the church abysmally fails to come to their rescue by refusing to confront their abusers. Of all the social problems bedeviling the Body of Christ, spousal abuse is one of the most virulent. Unfortunately, it is mostly misunderstood and mismanaged by church leaders, resulting in a high percentage of abused women no longer viewing the church as a source of help.

More often than not, pastors tell abused women that they should be more submissive to their abusive husbands, while other pastors simply counsel abused wives to remain in the marriage and trust God to take control of the untenable situation. Such pastors invariably invoke the Biblical injunction that wives ought to submit, even to abusive husbands, but submission does not stop abuse in its tracks. Rather, it often serves to intensify the abuse and gives the abusive husband a greater sense of power, ultimately helping him circumvent painful consequences for his evil behavior.

I share my story on behalf of all the *voiceless* women who are seemingly stuck in the mire of unrelenting abuse and who see no window of opportunity for escape in sight. I have never been an advocate of divorce or marital separation, nor did I ever envision that abuse and discord would spiral my marriage to the unfortunate place where it eventually ended. Finally able to gather what remained of my shredded wits and dignity, I decided to document my painful marital journey in the hope that my story will help some despairing woman out there fully comprehend her situation and take the necessary steps to remedy it by setting herself free from the shackles of abuse.

While I cannot share every detail of my saga, I share what is vital to help the bruised and broken among us. Your abuser's power lies in your silence. He counts on your reluctance to tell anyone about his wickedness and mediocre character. Secure in the belief that you dare not speak about what he is subjecting you to, and having established himself as your liege lord and master, he is convinced that your silence proves your total subjugation. He revels in his status as your tin god.

In dysfunctional homes all over the world, that *silence* is about to be broken so that this epidemic called *spousal abuse*, especially within the Body of Christ, can be exposed for the pernicious evil that it is. The abuser is sitting right beside you in church. His *"amen"* in response to prayer is the loudest in the congregation. He sings the most sonorous vocal notes in tandem with the choir at the high point of praise worship. He is quick to drop his offering into the collection basket, and when he is called to read the lesson, he does so with an authority that almost suggests that he authored the Bible. He is the quickest to volunteer to serve on church committees, and his constant refrain is that he is called to unhesitating service in the Lord's Vineyard, but the church only serves as a front for his near-demonic, savage, and authoritarian disposition at home. He may say he is a believer, but I call him the *silent killer and soul destroyer.* As I welcome you to the pages of this book, I urge you to approach its contents with a prayerful disposition and to withhold judgment of any sort, fully aware that you, the reader, may very well be next in line for spousal abuse. It is, after all, now a veritable epidemic within the Body of Christ. Happy reading.

Coach Dee L
Houston, Texas
December 2025

Chapter One
VOWS OF DECEPTION

"Happily ever after is not a fairy tale. It is a choice."

- FAWN WEAVER

Like most weddings, ours was beautiful. We were married on a fine Saturday morning, and throughout that day, my heart was filled with joy. Most brides are ecstatic on their wedding day, and my excitement was very evident; our parents spared no expense in giving us a fitting wedding.

I was no different from the average girl in my generation, and I had anticipated that my wedding day would signal the beginning of my *"happily ever after"* existence. Like most girls, my first glimpse of romance came from fairytales like *Cinderella*, and few educated women of my generation had not read the Mills and Boon or Barbara Cartland series and dreamed of marrying their own prince. By the time the average woman in my generation reached adolescence, she had already planned the details of her dream wedding with the hope of living happily ever after with her husband, just like the characters in the storybooks.

On my wedding day, I had my dream outfit, shoes, headdress, and everything else I had envisioned would transform me into a beautiful bride. As icing on my cake of joy, I was marrying the man I loved. We were joined together as husband and wife at the courthouse by an officiant who happened to be a pastor in one of the largest church organizations in Nigeria. We exchanged the traditional wedding vows: *"I, ______, take thee, ______, to be my wedded wife (husband), to have and to hold from this day forward, for better, for worse, for richer, for poorer, in sickness and in health, to love and to cherish, till death do us part."*

After the exchange of vows, we went to our church for the traditional church blessing, followed by a lavish wedding reception. The entire proceedings were picture-perfect, with nothing to suggest a less than perfect aftermath to a wonderful wedding ceremony. After the wedding, in accordance with the tradition of my people, the Yorúbá of Southwestern Nigeria, I returned home to receive parental blessings before being sent off with my husband. I remember my father telling me that night, as I knelt before him to receive his paternal blessings, to hold on to the Jesus I had accepted and not let go of Him. That was a totally unexpected statement, coming from a father who was a devout Muslim at the time. Although it remains within the realm of possibility that he was being sarcastic, it would ultimately turn out to be the best counsel anyone could have given me on that day. I still remember how my mother and I wept profusely and how my brother held me close to his heart that night as I cried. Understandably, my mother was absolutely terrified of what lay ahead of me in marriage, but my own thoughts were more rational. Admittedly, I was leaving the family I had known and loved for one that I certainly could not confidently say would offer me the comfort and affection I was accustomed to. However, I was marrying the man I loved and could only hope dearly that I would find happiness in my new home.

Marriage, as we all know, is an institution that is revered across all cultures. It symbolizes love, partnership, and commitment. Yet, its true meaning goes far beyond societal norms. At that early stage in my own marriage, my uncomplicated perspective was that the special bond I shared with the man I loved, and was now married to, embodied the epitome of love and commitment. In my estimation, my marriage signified the ultimate expression of my love and devotion, one through which

I had openly declared my commitment to my husband before family and friends. I truly felt a sense of security, believing I had a lifelong companion with whom I could now share life's joys and challenges. I saw marriage as a transformative journey of growth and compromise, and I was confident that we would learn from each other and embrace any necessary changes in personal perception. I believed that having a life partner would provide the pillar of strength with whom I could share both joy and sorrow, and I looked forward to a confidante who would listen to me, understand me, and stand by me during life's trials and triumphs.

As the famous saying goes, *"if wishes were horses, beggars would ride."* I would be jolted out of my dreams of an ideal future right from the night of my wedding. A husband is supposed to be a protector, a provider, and a pursuer. However, on the night of our wedding day, I received my first shock in what would turn out to be the beginning of an extremely tumultuous union, even as my expectation of protection was totally dashed. We had agreed that, as believers, we would refrain from dancing before the music band that was invited to entertain our guests. Naturally, I was secure in the belief that my husband had notified his family of our decision in this regard. As events would later prove, he did not. When it was time to dance, and I was invited to the dance floor, I was frantic. Although I was momentarily at a loss as to what to do in the circumstances, I was determined to honor my Savior and dance only before Him, and so I found myself fighting the battle all alone. I simply refused to go to the dance floor, even though I realized it was the most unpleasant way to start life with my new family. The man who promised to protect me, cherish me, and honor me was nowhere to be found. He had disappeared into thin air, leaving me to fight alone.

That was only the beginning of a journey of marital despair. It had been a beautiful wedding day, and most wedding days are beautiful and memorable. However, I was beginning to learn that even a fairytale wedding is no cast-iron guarantee of marital bliss. Love may be blind, but marriage quickly becomes the eye-opener, and although I felt so much pain at this sad disappointment, I quickly made excuses for my husband. There would be other disappointments, and many other departures from the spirit of our wedding vows, but that first night was the start of a series of disappointments that continually left me dumb with utter disbelief. The truth is that from that first day of our marriage, I went from one phase of marital horror to another. I had expected to be loved and cherished, but I was used and manipulated. At this early stage, I had no idea what was in store for me in an uncertain future, but the deed was done, and there was no going back. The vows were actually empty ones as, years later, I found out that he thought of opting out of the wedding and only went ahead because it appeared too late to cancel the arrangements. According to him, his best friend prevailed on him to go ahead with the wedding, and he did not want to deflate the balloon of happiness of a doting mother who had been looking forward to his wedding day.

Genesis 2:24 says, *"Therefore a man shall leave his father and mother and be joined to his wife, and they shall become one flesh."* I doubt these words had any significant meaning for my husband. He always chose his mother over me, and I constantly felt like I was playing second fiddle to her. Today, I wish he had canceled the wedding, as that would have spared me the horrors of marriage as I knew it. Marriage should be enjoyed, not endured, but the latter was my experience, as I suffered through every day of our joint existence as a couple. He claimed to love me at the beginning, but he was being completely disingenuous. *Why did he not just bow out of our plans to get married? Why did he proceed with a wedding that was nothing but a monument to deception? Whatever happened to the revelation he'd had that seemingly led him to me?* These, and many other questions, remained unanswered throughout my marriage. Ultimately, however, the foundation of deception was laid on our wedding day, and the deceit would only worsen as the years went by.

To this day, I am not quite sure why my husband did not cancel the wedding. My best guess is that he married me because he believed I would be a good source of support, and he was quite right about that. He likely also thought he had enough information about me to demean me, plunge me into guilt, threaten me, ridicule me, and ultimately manipulate me into submission. When all is said and done, my father's advice to hold on to Jesus proved invaluable at every stage of my traumatic marriage. Holding on to Jesus was what carried me through many painful days and nights. I shed many tears throughout my marriage, but Jesus never left me, and I learned to hold on to Him for dear life and comfort. The divine encounter that brought me to salvation was constantly replayed in my subconscious mind, helping me not to give up on my faith, despite my trials and challenges in marriage.

CHAPTER TWO
HONEYMOON BLUES

"Marriage is Hard. Divorce is Hard. Choose your hard."

- LOUISA ALCOTT

In Nigerian society, marriage is a highly exalted concept that comes with hopes and dreams of living happily ever after with a husband and beautiful children. Marriage is every woman's dream, and women are prepared for it from when they are little girls. Regrettably, no one educates these girls on the challenges that come with marriage. The entire concept of marriage, which is the exclusive and monogamous union of a man and a woman grounded in a commitment to mutual love, and with the intent to sustain that commitment until death, is so elevated that unmarried women often feel unaccomplished and out of place in a society that places an unreasonably high premium on marriage. In Nigerian society, as soon as a woman attains a certain age but is not married, or there is no talk of imminent marriage in her overall narrative, she is considered unworthy of respect and esteem. She comes under undue pressure from parents who feel compelled to meet society's expectations for them to become in-laws to another family.

In my opinion, if the Nigerian society had the opportunity to rewrite the first few verses of 1 Corinthians 13 specifically for women, it would probably read as follows:

"If I can speak ten different tongues, and if I have the gift of eloquence, yet I have no husband, I am nothing but the noise from an empty vessel. If I open my mouth to speak, and people are inspired all over the world, and if I acquire a huge mansion, yet I have no husband, I am nothing. If I do charitable works, and if I work very hard to build a worthy life for myself, but I have no husband, I have achieved nothing. No matter what I accomplish, I am bankrupt and pathetic without a husband."

Consequently, instead of feeling accomplished with all the beautiful things that life has to offer, unmarried women languish in self-pity because they are without husbands. Ultimately, having a husband has been elevated to the point of worship, with many women believing that having a husband is what defines them. It is what many live for and strive to obtain at any cost, but that should not be the case for two good reasons. *Firstly*, not every one of us is called to the institution of marriage. *Secondly*, each of us has dreams, and while dreams are great and provide hope for a glorious future, they do not always come true. Unfortunately, I belong to the second category; I had dreamt of a happy home with a loving husband, but it turned out to be just that: a dream, and one that would not come true.

We left for our honeymoon the day after the wedding, but we had to settle for a brief honeymoon because we did not have sufficient money for a longer one. We managed our resources prudently and returned home after a week. During our honeymoon, we spent most of the time discussing what kind of home we wanted, but with the wisdom of hindsight, our conversations were lopsided, with my husband asking me many questions about what he would later term my *"bad past."* At that time, I thought his questions were borne out of curiosity, but I now know better. When an abuser questions you, the goal is to gather information they can use against you at the appropriate time. At the beginning of our relationship, I had told him about my family, my upbringing, and my past relationships, and during the honeymoon, he inquired about all those things, and I provided answers. He appeared to appreciate my candor and honesty, but little did I know that my virtue of honesty would become something he detested, particularly when he was caught lying and I challenged him.

Unfortunately, telling my husband everything about me turned out to be one of the greatest mistakes in my marriage, as all that I shared, including my family history, would later become an encumbrance used against me at every turn throughout our marriage. He would incessantly talk about the things I told him about my family and use them to insult me. Shamelessly breaching all known boundaries of confidentiality and divulging matters I shared with him in secret, my husband went as far as discussing my family with third parties in a bid to justify his mistreatment of me. It took me a long time to realize that my secrets were not safe with him, and eventually, I stopped sharing anything he could use as a reason for demeaning me.

Nothing is quite as difficult as dealing with an *angry* and *bitter* man. My husband was both. Unfortunately, there is no manual that teaches one how to deal with such men, and I had to navigate the waters based on what I knew. The Bible enjoins us in Hebrews 12:15 not to allow the root of bitterness to defile us, but despite the solace I took in that scripture, I watched helplessly as my husband became more and more bitter in our marriage with each passing day. He would call me names, including *"ashewo,"* Nigerian local parlance for prostitute, and while that insult is no longer hurtful, it is bothersome as no child of God should be described in such a derogatory manner, much less addressed as such regularly. He would also call me *"oniranu,"* local parlance for '*aimless person*.' Yet, each time he called me names, God would assure me that I was His child and that I was accepted in the *beloved,"****....to the praise of the glory of His grace, by which He made us accepted in the Beloved." (Ephesians 1:6).*** Throughout my marriage, God's words remained reassuring and comforting, and I am grateful to God for the genuine solace I have found in His words. With the benefit of hindsight, my advice to any child of God is to be mindful of what they share about their past and their family with their spouse or anyone else, for that matter.

The immediate post-honeymoon phase of marriage seeks true meaning in the celebration of love and unity. For me, that phase breached every known notion of affection and bonding, and rather than deepen our emotional connection to lay the foundation for a strong and resilient partnership, the threats and demeaning remarks would start, and within a month, my husband would be threatening me with divorce. Shortly after we returned from our honeymoon, my woes began, and it was almost as if our marriage ended during the honeymoon period.

It was in the third week of our marriage that I first experienced my husband's rage, which grew worse as the days went by. One morning, I said something to my husband that he considered an insult and an affront to his ego. He took instant offense and *lashed out at me.* Although I was in utter shock, that was merely the beginning of my ordeal. Insulting me to his heart's content, he called me all sorts of names before storming out of the house. We were only three weeks into our marriage, and I was already dealing with rage. I sat still, totally downcast. Some might say they would have left the marriage immediately. In reality, however, would they have? One can only imagine my consternation, hurt, and confusion as I wept profusely. To this day, I have no idea where he went after storming out, but while he was gone, I prayed and cried until I had no tears left to shed. He did not return until later in the evening, and when he did, appearing full of remorse, he apologized.

Regrettably, the rage of that day was a mere foretaste of the living hell and verbal abuse that I would endure throughout my marriage. The rage continued, as did the insults and constant barrage of abusive words. Most of the time, I countered with no words of my own and resorted to prayer instead. My recourse to prayer was primarily due to the pain I experienced. At one point, the pain became extremely intense, and I was divinely led to start writing. That was when I wrote my first book, *"Thinking out Loud - Thoughts from the Book of Genesis."* The book is a devotional, and I noted therein that it was written *"in the quiet crucible of my personal pain and sufferings."*

My husband always accused me of being talkative, using that as an excuse to shut down and silence me. For days, and sometimes weeks, he would simply refuse to engage in any meaningful conversation with me while constantly raining abusive words on me. I had always believed that only women descended to that level of pettiness, but I soon learned that some men, including my husband, are petty. *How does a man marry a woman and simply refuse to talk to her?* I was baffled, and in my confusion, I sought communication with him, sometimes begging him to talk to me. His response was always that there was nothing to discuss and that he was done with me. He discontinued family devotion and would tell me to go and have devotion by myself. Even when we started having children, family devotion was a struggle. If I did not initiate it, we simply did not have morning devotion, as he would rather sleep than pray with us.

The abusive words became the norm in the landscape of our marriage, and my children grew up familiar with them, his favorite being "*Ashewo.*" The one thing that stood out throughout our marriage, besides the constant deluge of abusive words, was the silent treatment, which I later learned is an abuser's most formidable weapon. It leaves you confused and vulnerable. My husband was a master at it, using it to maximum effect. By the time we were barely a month into the marriage, he was obviously done with me and started threatening to divorce me, insisting it was only a matter of time before he did. I remembered my father's words on my wedding night to hold on to my faith, and I was determined to fight for my marriage and win my husband over. Sadly, despite fasting, praying, and trusting God, matters only grew worse.

It is now more than 30 years since we got married, and I still haven't won my husband over. Rather than change, he has become a monster who seizes every opportunity to demean me. He has been on a smear campaign against me for years, and I have been forced to defend myself and attempt to repair my damaged image, but not without much pain. There have been times when I thought of leaving, but one of the things that prevented me was, *"What would be my testimony to my Muslim family?* "A brother told me only recently that I must get to the point where I can say, *"Who cares what the world will say?"* It is possible that if I had embraced that notion years ago, I would not have worried about what my family would say. Many women remain in abusive marriages just because of what people will say, but, "*Is it worth it?* "To be honest, when a woman loves a man, it can be difficult to give up and let go of the relationship. Bearing children makes it even harder because you don't want your children to end up as products of a broken home. As a young girl, I witnessed the struggles of my friends from broken homes, and I wasn't willing to put my children through that struggle.

I always hoped for a happy ending to my story, but many years later, I now realize that not everyone lives happily ever after. Besides, *happily ever after* is merely a storybook concept. For anyone, male or female, dealing with severe spousal abuse, I suggest that you should not stay on a ship when it is sinking. Cast your mind back to the tragedy of the Titanic and how many of its passengers might have been saved if they had abandoned the ship early enough. Saving yourself and your children should be of utmost importance and your number one priority. Jesus has already paid the price, so there is no reason for us to pay any other price. Since He laid down His life, we do not have to lay down ours. However, it is up to each person to choose what is best for them in their circumstances. I tell my story so that anyone experiencing abuse will have a deeper understanding of its impact on them and their children, and I hope that my story will help someone take the right steps in the right direction. Every covenant has a path, and that path is not traversed by the distracted, the casual, or the spiritually indifferent.

CHAPTER THREE

VERBAL TIRADES

"If the words or attitude disempower, disrespect, or devalue the other, then they are abusive."

- PATRICIA EVANS

1 Peter 4:8 encourages us to have fervent love for one another, because *"love will cover a multitude of sins."* Unfortunately, love was absent in my marriage. Despite my efforts to love my husband and overlook his appalling behavior, nothing changed; the cycle of abuse continued and worsened. Few would have believed my husband was abusive, as he presented himself as a quiet, peace-loving person to those outside our home. However, this was a façade, cultivated over the years. One of his friends even described him as a perfect gentleman in college, but in reality, he was anything but that.

To the world, he was a saint, but to his family, he was a monster. At home, we faced the brunt of his anger at every turn. He was unhappy with nearly everyone, yet few outside our immediate family were aware of his rage. My first experience of this, just three weeks into our marriage, should have prepared me for the difficult times ahead, but I mistakenly believed it was an isolated incident. I failed to see that his rage was an intrinsic part of who he was. Though I would eventually uncover the truth behind the gentlemanly façade, I was entirely unprepared for the verbal tirades that awaited me.

His favorite term for me was *"ashewo,"* the Yorúbá word for prostitute. I lived under constant suspicion, as he repeatedly accused me of infidelity. Engaging in conversation with another man, even in church, would trigger his jealousy. He kept me under relentless surveillance; if I was away from home, he would call incessantly to confirm I was where I said I would be. Eventually, I recognized this surveillance for what it was and stopped answering his calls.

One day, I got caught in traffic, and when I finally returned home, the rage I encountered was unimaginable. He accused me of visiting my boyfriend. Nothing could have been further from the truth; I remained faithful to my marriage vows, even amid his harshness. Visiting friends became a nightmare, as I was accused of flirting with the men in their homes. Eventually, I began to decline joint visits and opted to go alone instead.

My life quickly turned into hell, especially after we had children. I did everything I could to please him, yet the abuse continued unabated. Not a week went by without insults, and nothing I did was ever good enough. He constantly disrespected and belittled me, once even telling me I should be grateful he married me and that I ought to "worship" him for being so "gracious." This demand was absurd, and while I never conceded to him, I found it strange that he *expected worship* from me. To my understanding, only God is worthy of worship. Later, I learned that a "God Complex" is often associated with abusers who have narcissistic personality disorder, especially if they harbor grandiose beliefs about their power over others. Although his demand for worship was shocking, I kept my thoughts to myself.

I was not a perfect wife—no one can truly claim perfection in marriage. However, I am certain I was a good and supportive partner, yet nothing I did was ever sufficient for him. His incessant criticism buried me in a relentless avalanche of words, transforming the torrent of verbal abuse into a disturbing norm in our lives. My grief was indescribable. Constantly drowning in unkind and scathing remarks wore me down, and I began to lose myself. My thoughts spiraled out of control, and I felt as if I was experiencing a complete hostile takeover. My husband often kept me up at night, throwing tantrums over minor issues from the day. I found myself compelled to explain my actions in the middle of the night. Eventually, I realized it was unreasonable for someone with a job to stay awake all night responding to his inquiries. At that point, *I finally said, "If you didn't bring it up during the day, then it can wait."*

Standing up for myself often led to more demeaning behavior from my husband, but I learned to cope with his outbursts by simply walking away. There were days when I yelled back, but as one might imagine, that only made things worse. The scripture in 2 Corinthians 5:17 tells us that if anyone is in Christ, he is a new creation, yet nothing in my husband's actions suggested he had undergone any transformation. He presented a baffling paradox; he claimed to be *"born again,"* yet every day, the only thing that seemed renewed was his inclination for conflict and hostility in our marriage. I often felt like I was living with the *devil* himself and wondered what had happened to the man I married.

One undeniable truth was that he was toxic and abusive. His verbal assaults—derogatory name-calling, harsh criticism, and other insults—slowly eroded my already fragile self-esteem. Even when he appeared less vicious, he would mask his abuse with biting sarcasm or cruel jokes. My husband's verbal abuse was devastating; he was a skilled manipulator who wore me down with his relentless tirades. To make matters worse, he twisted the narrative to make it seem as though his abusive behavior was my fault, successfully intimidating me and asserting his misguided sense of dominance.

His behavior, especially early in our marriage, followed the typical pattern of an abuser. Verbal attacks were often followed by shallow apologies. As time passed, he began using the volume and tone of his voice to establish control. When enraged, his tone was both domineering and pompous. He would rage and yell, then switch to a strategy of complete silence, ignoring me entirely and dismissing all my attempts to communicate. My husband wielded words as weapons to instill fear, intimidate, manipulate, and oppress me. He would interrupt me in a bullying manner, and his rapid verbal assaults left me too drained to respond. To further complicate matters, he skillfully blended truth with falsehood, leaving me confused and defeated. Ultimately, the barrage of verbal insults shattered my self-esteem and self-confidence, making me feel as if I were always walking on eggshells.

Although I often wondered what had gone wrong, I eventually realized that it all stemmed from his wounded ego, which was bruised by the fact that he was not the first man in my life. Unfortunately, verbal abuse became the norm in our home, and its frequency taught me to *tune it out.* Thankfully, I discovered an outlet for my frustration when God guided me to baking and decorating cakes. This creative pursuit distracted me from the trauma and provided me with a sense of stability. Upon arriving in the United States, I needed to work. My job, coupled with my passion for cake-making, allowed me to focus on something beyond the abuse. My children and friends at work also brought me joy, and I often pondered what I would have done without a job. Throughout it all, God remained faithful, helping me maintain my sanity. I held on to my father's advice to cling to Jesus, and that is exactly what I did. In the midst of all the trauma I endured, Jesus became my only true friend, and the lyrics of the song *"I've found a friend in Jesus..."* took on new meaning during my turbulent marriage.

CHAPTER FOUR

REGIMENTAL SUBMISSION

"The Christian life is about serving each other. It is not about controlling any other person or demanding obedience. In fact, if anyone does that, then they are acting in an unchristian manner. They are not reflecting God; they are reflecting the enemy. Therefore, your husband should not control you, and he is acting unbiblically if he does."

- SHEILA WRAY GREGOIRE

Life was difficult in every sense, including financially, amid the tension in my relationship with my husband. I did everything I could to shield my children from what was happening. While I worked hard to conceal his behavior, my husband seemed determined to exert total control over me, using various tactics to instill fear and subjugation. A young lady once remarked that, after observing how my husband addressed and treated me, she wondered who this "lord and master" was. That observation perfectly captured the situation in my home, and for many years, I allowed the "good girl" syndrome to keep me captive.

To illustrate the domestic dynamic accurately, here is a typical exchange between my husband and me.

"Good afternoon," I greeted him warmly upon returning from a nearby store.

He offered no response, staring blankly into space.

"Is everything okay?" I asked, fully aware that he was simply being his usual petulant self.

"Is there a reason for things to not be okay?" he finally snapped, visibly angry as always.

"I'm sorry. I was just curious as to why you didn't respond to my greeting," I replied, my heart racing as I carefully navigated the fragile situation.

"I have nothing to say to you, "he retorted with palpable hostility.

"What on Earth did I do this time?" I asked, feeling helpless.

"What did you not do?" My husband *hissed angrily. "Oniranu! Where have you been?"* (You may recall that *"oniranu"* is *Yoruba for "aimless person.")*

"I only went to the store. I don't understand why you're so angry, but God will deliver me," I responded quietly and calmly.

His fury intensified.

"I'm the one who needs to be delivered from you, ashewo! Your foolishness growing up has messed up your life, and I have to deal with it. Nonsense! How many men would tolerate the nonsense I put up with from you every day? When we get to Heaven, even God will commend me for enduring all this."

I sighed and walked to the kitchen to put away the groceries.

This conversation was just one of many painful exchanges in our home, which felt less like a sanctuary and more like a battleground.

With my husband, it was all about power and control. To justify his relentless pursuit of my subjugation, he wielded the scripture in Ephesians 5:22 like a weapon. During our marriage, the verse, *"Wives, submit to your own husbands, as to the Lord,"* became his *anthem of* oppression. Like many men of his kind, he twisted this noble Biblical instruction, conveniently ignoring the corresponding command that husbands should love their wives as Christ loved the church, as stated in Ephesians 5:*25: "Husbands, love your wives, just as Christ also loved the church and gave Himself for her."* While I did submit, it was a forced submission that resembled total subjugation more than anything else.

He would angrily storm around the house, constantly reminding me that he was my husband and the head of the family. Unfortunately, he not only refused to follow the biblical injunction that husbands should love their wives as Christ loved the church, but he also completely neglected his responsibility to provide for the family he claimed to lead. In his distorted view, my husband believed that part of loving me meant keeping me subjugated and punishing or disciplining me as he saw fit. His treatment of me was extremely harsh and domineering, and he saw nothing wrong with it, despite the teaching that we are supposed to be *equal before God.*

In Genesis 2:18, God declared, *"It is not good for the man to be alone. I will make a helper suitable for him."* But does *"suitable helper"* imply that the woman was created to be a *servant* to the man, or does *it* suggest that the man should trample upon the woman? Does it indicate that the man should lord over the woman to the point of disrespecting her? The answers to these questions are a resounding *"No!"* The term "helper" does not imply lesser authority; rather, the woman is intended to assist the man as his equal. The message in Genesis is clear: the woman is *"suitable"* for the man, sharing the same essence.

Furthermore, the text emphasizes that the man is incomplete without the woman. There is no mention of authority in this verse. The Apostle Paul also recognized the mutual dependence of men and *women, stating, "Nevertheless, neither is man independent of woman, nor woman independent of man, in the Lord" (1 Corinthians 11:11).* There is no reference to inferiority or hierarchy. God caused the man to sleep, took one of his ribs, and fashioned a woman from it, highlighting her *organic* unity with him. When God brought the woman to the man, *he exclaimed, "This is now bone of my bones and flesh of my flesh; she shall be called 'woman,' for she was taken out of man."* This poetic declaration expressed his joy at finding the suitable partner he needed. Although different, they were of the same flesh.

Thousands of years later, despite the male-dominated culture of His time, Jesus treated women with respect and kindness. He was sensitive to their needs and often highlighted women as examples of faith, including them in His ministry in significant ways. He interacted with women frequently and was first seen by them after His resurrection. Overall, Jesus never belittled women; instead, He presented them as positive role models of faith for men to emulate.

In my husband's eyes, I had no value whatsoever. He would even question what about me was worthy of respect. When I cried out of frustration and despair, it only fueled his anger, leading him to suggest that my tears were nothing more than crocodile tears. Although this is clearly a form of emotional abuse, many women fail to recognize it as such. My husband would often say things like, *"You are arrogant, and the Bible says you should submit to your husband."* Yet, I struggled to identify any way in which I had not submitted to him. I not only submitted myself but also submitted everything I owned to my name in an effort to maintain peace. Still, he continued to distance himself from me and neglect my emotional needs. My advice to anyone reading this book is to be cautious of a man who uses the Bible to control you; it could indicate deeper issues.

I constantly walked on eggshells, mostly remaining silent out of fear of his rage. I was not a fool; I simply chose peace over conflict. Occasionally, when I reacted to his cruelty, he would dismiss me and use my response to label me as rebellious, claiming I was teaching rebellion to other women in church and disrupting the house of God. When I confided in his best friend about my struggles, he pointed out that in Proverbs 31, the man merely sat at the gates, suggesting I should swallow my pride and do what was necessary to keep the peace. Myles Munroe once said, *"Don't trust a man without a* head," and I fully agree with this advice. No man should ever outgrow submission to authority, yet my husband had no one *above him* to correct or counsel him. A man without accountability is one of the most dangerous types; where there is no oversight, danger looms on the horizon, and disaster is inevitable.

I desperately wanted to save my marriage, but the threat of divorce loomed constantly. My husband made it clear that he wished to end our relationship, openly expressing his preference for other women. However, I was his financial support, which made the idea of leaving me unappealing. Our conversations revolved solely around his desires, with little regard for mine. He only pretended to be kind when he wanted something from me or when we were in public, where he felt the need to maintain a facade. For years, I failed to recognize his manipulation and gaslighting for what they truly were.

I continuously made excuses for him because I loved him and valued my marital commitment. In return, I faced snide remarks, disrespect, and isolation. Whenever he needed something from me—especially money—

he showered me with affection, complimenting my beauty and professing his love until he got his way. If his romantic advances didn't succeed, he resorted to bullying or pleading to compel my compliance. He would bring me the cheapest flowers, which I found more insulting than not receiving any at all. Complaining about the wilting flowers only earned me labels of ingratitude and name-calling. It became easier to simply say thank you and move on. Ultimately, I received beautiful floral arrangements from women at church, which made up for the withering ones from him. I even began buying myself flowers to lift my spirits.

Everything he did was aimed at conquering and subduing me. To secure my peace, I often gave in to his many demands. He had access to all my information, which I granted because I believed in Genesis 2:*25: "And they were both naked, the man and his wife, and were not ashamed."* This verse symbolizes mutual *openness* and *honesty.* However, Amos 3:3 *states, "Can two walk together, unless they are agreed?"* indicating that agreement is necessary for unity. Unfortunately, my husband and I were far from aligned. While I sought unity, he sought control. The more information I shared, the more ammunition he had to subdue me, all while disguising his intentions under Ephesians 5:22, which *calls for a woman's submission. I often wondered why, despite my submission, he did not love me as Ephesians*

5:25 instructs. What about Ephesians 5:21, which calls for mutual submission in the fear of God? I realized he saw himself as lord and master, rather than allowing Jesus to be the true Lord of our home.

By choosing to avoid confrontation and prioritize peace at any cost, I unknowingly empowered my husband to continue his manipulative behavior. I failed to set appropriate boundaries, inadvertently encouraging him to treat me poorly. As a result, I became an unwitting supporter of his abhorrent conduct. Despite being married, I felt incredibly alone, and the entire situation was a disaster. To say he enjoyed my complete capitulation would be an understatement.

If you are reading this and find yourself in a situation even remotely similar to mine, understand this: by surrendering and maintaining your silence, you contribute to your own destruction. It may be time to reevaluate your position in your marriage and establish necessary boundaries.

Chapter Five

THE SLAVE WIFE

"The woman was made of a rib out of the side of Adam; not made out of his head to rule over him, nor out of his feet to be trampled upon by him, but out of his side to be equal with him, under his arm to be protected, and near his heart to be beloved."

- MATTHEW HENRY

From the very beginning, my husband exhibited a strong sense of entitlement that diminished my status as a partner. He often reminded me that he was the *head* of the family, and though he didn't say it outright, he made it clear that I was expected to serve him as if he were the lord and master of our household. Early in our marriage, he developed a habit of removing his shoes, socks, tie, and shirt in the living room and leaving them there, expecting me to pick them up. This behavior starkly illustrated my role as his glorified servant. At first, I didn't mind cleaning up after him; I saw it as a warm expression of my affection for him. However, the underlying, cynical motive behind his actions became increasingly apparent, and I soon realized I could no longer play the demeaning role he had imposed on me.

Sadly, to my husband, I was little more than property to be used and discarded at his convenience. Fortunately, the Bible clearly defines a woman's role in marriage. Women are called to be supportive partners, not *servants. As stated in Genesis 2:18, "And the Lord God said, 'It is not good that man should be alone; I will make him a helper comparable to him.'"* Matthew Henry, a biblical commentator, *elaborates, "The woman was made of a rib out of the side of Adam; not made out of his head to rule over him, nor out of his feet to be trampled upon by him, but out of his side to be equal with him, under his arm to be protected, and near his heart to be beloved."*

I was expected to be seen and not heard. On the rare occasions I dared to express my opinion, he would respond with anger, reminding me in a *harsh tone, "I am the husband, and I will not allow you to tell me what to do."* I knew his attitude was completely contrary to God's intention for a married couple, but I felt powerless to change it.

My husband was not only ominously entitled but also extremely paranoid, with his low self-esteem driving him to assert control over me even when it was unnecessary.

This behavior was a classic manifestation of an abuser. Typically, abusers struggle with low self-esteem and deep insecurity, masking their vulnerabilities with a façade of superiority, bravado, and entitlement. Naively, I played along, believing I was following the directive of Ephesians 5:25 by submitting to him in all respects. I often bit my tongue and surrendered to his tantrums to maintain peace and protect my children from punishment for my imagined "misdeeds," a topic for another time.

The church teachings at that time did not alleviate the situation. The pulpit frequently proclaimed that *submission* was the ultimate solution for achieving peace in the home. Interestingly, this message was promoted by two distinct groups. The *first* consisted of men, likely authoritarian figures in *their own homes, and the second* comprised older women who preached submission as a virtue without sharing their *own struggles. These "veterans of the home* front" were quick to highlight how Sarah referred to her husband as "Lord," and I admit I subscribed to that outdated belief, much to my detriment. My husband exploited these teachings to manipulate and control me. It took me many years to realize that an abusive partner gradually grooms you into their *slave* and *puppet* without you even noticing.

I was *a cook, cleaner, nanny,* and provider all in one. Yet, my efforts were never enough for my husband; he desired more than just submission. When I lived in Nigeria, household chores felt manageable because I could afford domestic help. In the United States, however, my limited income made that luxury impossible. Beyond submission, my husband demanded servitude, and when I fell short, I faced abuse and criticism. Nothing I did was ever satisfactory, and even the rare moments of praise quickly dissolved into more verbal abuse. He constantly reminded me that it was my duty to manage the household and clean the house, which I did—often staying up late to complete chores. I was already a night owl; when I started my cake business, nighttime became my baking time. It was also my time with God, where I worshipped and prayed while creating and decorating cakes, and God blessed my work immensely.

Like any slave, I was the last to go to bed and the first to rise in the morning. Sometimes I was called upon for marital duties, and if I failed to show up or accidentally fell asleep, I faced the full force of his rage the next day. I admit that the marital landscape was not always bleak. There were moments when I found a silver lining amidst the clouds of anger—times when he sought something from me, showering me with compliments and laughter in a bid to win me over. Unfortunately, these moments were merely manipulative tactics to force my submission. Psychological abuse is more damaging than physical violence; it gnaws at the very core of your being, and that was my experience. Over time, I became a shadow of my former self, the once-vibrant *Wura* losing her confidence and self-esteem, all while no one knew the pain I endured day and night. I wore a smile out of shame, too embarrassed to share my story. I walked with my head held high as if I had everything under control, but no one could see the shame I carried. I did what I needed to present a façade to the world, yet it is difficult to convey the anguish that plagued me.

I want to emphasize that submission, as a Biblical principle, is not inherently wrong. However, it should not be ***misconstrued as servitude*** or used as a means of control. Ephesians 5:17-21 calls us to be wise, filled with the Spirit, and to submit to one another. In this context, submission should be mutual, not one-sided. Furthermore, a husband must love his wife as Christ loves the church. Therefore, when a man demands submission, he must also be ready to love his wife selflessly, even to the point of sacrifice. I urge any man reading this to understand that it is this Christlike love that enables a woman to submit willingly and without hesitation.

According to an article from Florida State College titled, *"Life As A Slave In The Cotton Kingdom,"* slaveholders used both psychological coercion and physical violence to ensure compliance among slaves. Regrettably, my story mirrors that of those slaves on cotton plantations. My husband waged relentless psychological warfare against me, manipulating a largely misunderstood Biblical narrative on submission, while constantly threatening divorce. I was a wife, yet I was treated like a slave.

I loved to sing, but for a long time, I couldn't sing Yorùbá songs because my husband would get angry and rage against it. He did not want me singing Yorùbá songs in our home. Eventually, I began to defy him, singing to my heart's content. I remember one instance when I sang the *hymn "Fill My Cup, Lord." When I reached the line, "fill me till I want no more,"* my husband became furious, questioning why I wouldn't want more of the Holy Spirit. My explanation that I was simply repeating the song's lyrics made no difference to him, so I had to ask the Holy Spirit for alternative words to appease him. Fortunately, the Holy Spirit provided, and I started singing that line as *"Fill me till I overflow."*

My husband craved the authority of a king while only accepting accountability suited for a toddler. He was an actor who had mastered his craft, but no one, including myself, recognized the reality behind his facade. I chose not to speak about my abuser or the abuse itself, which allowed him to continue his performance undetected. He began calling me *Vashti* and acting out the role of King Ahasuerus in his own absurd drama. He repeatedly insisted that I was Vashti and should leave, yet I remained, hoping for a change in his behavior and believing it would come. Eventually, I realized who I was truly dealing with and understood that my husband would not change. His mindset was entirely contrary to scripture, and even when God told him he wasn't treating me well, nothing improved. Someone once said, based on the story of Joseph, *"If you cannot see your family members as prime ministers, you will put them in the pit."* This was true for my husband, who saw me not as a valued partner but as someone easily cast into the pit of abuse. Deuteronomy 24:1 states that if a man marries a woman and dislikes her, he should divorce her; however, my husband could not do that. To divorce me would mean losing the benefits he derived from my family and me, so he kept me while subjecting me to ongoing abuse and mistreatment.

Chapter Six
COMING TO AMERICA

"Speak up, because the day you don't speak up for the things that matter to you is the day your freedom truly ends."

- DR. MARTIN LUTHER KING JR.

When we started raising a family, I felt it was crucial to be present for my children, so I chose to be a stay-at-home mom. Despite working at a prestigious law firm with a good income, I was willing to sacrifice that for the sake of my children, and fortunately, my husband supported my decision. However, I did not anticipate the financial challenges that would come with a single-income household. To compensate for my lost income, I explored various businesses, including butchering and selling different products, but the returns were insufficient to meet our family's needs. At that point, I realized I needed divine intervention.

Our financial struggles worsened when my husband left his law firm job to start his own legal practice, a decision that seemed misguided since he lacked an established clientele. Although I should have opposed his decision, he was adamant that God called him to this new venture. As a supportive wife, I felt I had no choice but to agree. Unfortunately, business was slow, and the practice could not sustain us. In prayer, I sought God's guidance, and He instructed me to start baking cakes for a living. As an attorney, baking was not something I would have considered, but God's ways are beyond *human understanding. "Oh, the depth of the riches both of the wisdom and knowledge of God! How unsearchable are His judgments and His ways past finding out!" (Romans 11:33).*

Initially, my cake business had few customers, but over time, God granted me valuable insights into baking and cake decorating, leading to a surprising increase in clientele and a significant improvement in our financial situation. My cake business thrived, eventually allowing me to become the primary breadwinner. Throughout our struggles, I remained loyal to my husband. Sadly, it became evident that he felt threatened by my success, often expressing his frustration by saying God was blessing me and that I was the provider, even though our circumstances were not of my making.

In the midst of our struggles and despair, God revealed His generous hand. *"He lifted me out of the slimy pit, out of the mud and mire; he set my feet on a rock and gave me a firm place to stand." (Psalm 40:2).* A miracle, aided by my cousin's efforts, allowed me to win the American visa lottery, and we began the process of relocating to the United States. However, when it was time to leave Nigeria, we couldn't afford the airfare. Thankfully, my mother stepped in and covered the cost of plane tickets for our entire family.

I hoped that moving to America would provide relief from my marital troubles, and I was determined to work hard to make my marriage succeed. Yet, I could not have been more mistaken. Despite my history of shattered hopes, I clung to optimism, reminiscent of Abraham in *Romans 4:18, "who, contrary to hope, in hope believed, so that he became the father of many nations, according to what was spoken, 'So shall your descendants be.'"* I had nurtured the hope that winning the lottery would inspire my husband to treat me kindly, and that our relationship would improve, but I was gravely disappointed.

Upon arriving in the United States, we stayed with friends who were incredibly kind to us and our children. We found a church and became devoted members of the congregation, secretly believing that being part of a strong church community would improve our marital situation.

Regrettably, my hopes were once again dashed as nothing changed; in fact, things worsened. It felt as though I had jumped from the frying pan into the fire, yet I remained silent about my struggles. I continued to bake and decorate cakes, which not only provided an escape but also helped us earn extra money to pay the bills, especially since my husband was frequently unemployed until he eventually quit working altogether to pursue full-time ministry. Those who encountered us at church might have assumed we were the epitome of marital bliss, as we often presented ourselves as the perfect couple in matching outfits. I intentionally chose our Sunday attire in hopes of endearing my husband to me, but my efforts proved fruitless. I expected him to appreciate my creativity, but it meant nothing to him, even after we arrived in the United States. Ultimately, the matching outfits became a farce and a complete waste of resources.

My American journey quickly descended into unfathomable trauma, as experiences I had not even faced in Nigeria began to unfold in the U.S. Without an accountability partner, my husband acted as he pleased. With no one to report him to, his rage and anger remained unchecked. Often, after spending the night insulting and dehumanizing me, he would drive to my workplace the next day to apologize. His greatest fear was that I would leave him, as evident in his desperate pleas for me to stay. He knew that I would always forgive him, often telling me that, unlike him, I was kind and forgiving. Yet, the very next day after my forgiveness, he would revert to his obnoxious behavior. He would insult me directly and send me abusive text messages to shame me. When I confronted him about his behavior, he would claim that I brought it on myself, despite it being a mere figment of his imagination.

The cycle of abuse and apology was truly unbelievable, persisting for many years until I finally recognized the reality of my situation and decided to establish necessary boundaries after enduring prolonged suffering in my marriage. In America, making friends became increasingly difficult because my husband preferred it that way. He frequently complained about my friends or claimed to have visions about them that instilled fear in me, causing me to withdraw. If I received a phone call, I had to disclose who was calling and the subject of the conversation so he could ensure I *wasn't "in the company of friends who would corrupt me"* or encourage me to *"elope with another man."* I have never had bad friends, nor has the thought of eloping with another man ever crossed my mind.

Despite his ongoing obnoxious behavior, I remained loyal to my husband and upheld my marriage vows. Regrettably, his constant fear of me leaving him for another man reflected his profound insecurity, leading to unfounded accusations of infidelity. If I had known what I understand now, I would have chosen myself and my children over a tumultuous marriage that broke me in every sense of the word, stripping me of any remaining dignity.

Eventually, we were called to pastor a church, and despite my zeal in supporting my husband and investing all my savings into the ministry, he continued to despise me. I loved God with all my heart and dedicated myself to His service, but my husband wielded fear as a weapon to keep me subjugated, even within the ministry. He often reminded me that authority should not be challenged. While I found this amusing, I recognized it was an attempt to control me, and he succeeded. One might wonder why a church leader would act so wickedly toward their spouse or anyone else, but God grants us the freedom to choose, never imposing His will on His children. Saul was chosen to be the king of Israel, yet he chose disobedience. Moreover, the gifts and calling of God are irrevocable (Romans 11:29). To many, including our family and friends, we appeared to be devoted believers and a model Christian couple. However, behind closed doors, we were far from that idealized image, and our arguments were endless.

In the early stages of our marriage, I was quite docile, but at some point, I began to stand up for myself, refusing to tolerate certain behaviors any longer. This was not an easy journey. Visitors to our home would likely find a Christian program playing on our TV. However, despite my husband's enthusiasm for these programs, they had no positive impact on our marriage, nor did the many Christian books he purchased, read, and lent to others to showcase his spirituality. With the benefit of hindsight, I now realize that my silence about my experiences was my greatest mistake, though I didn't see it then. Driven by love, I believed I was protecting my husband and our marriage while hiding my shame. Little did I know that for an abusive partner, silence is often seen as consent, signaling that their bad behavior is acceptable when, in truth, it is not.

Now that I understand abuse and its dynamics, I strongly encourage anyone facing similar circumstances to speak up instead of remaining complicit in their own suffering. You don't have to endure an endless cycle of trauma; you can take steps to free yourself now.

Chapter Seven

ONE LONG WINTER NIGHT

"I've learned that people will forget what you said, people will forget what you did, but people will never forget how you made them feel."

- MAYA ANGELOU

As I mentioned in the introduction, this book chronicles the events of my troubled marriage. However, it is nearly impossible to share every detail of my story. The experience I am about to recount is one of the most painful moments in my marriage. Although I have forgiven my husband, the memory of that night remains vivid. When I reflect on those events, I am reminded of Maya Angelou's words: *"I've learned that people will forget what you said, people will forget what you did, but people will never forget how you made them feel."* To this day, I have not forgotten how my husband made me feel that night. I have shared this story with a few close friends, but to my dismay, they have chosen not to confront my husband about his behavior. I will address the role of my friends in another chapter.

It was a Wednesday evening, and we were headed to church after a snowy day. Throughout the afternoon, I had endured the *silent treatment* from my husband, but we were still going to ride to church together. No sooner had we entered the car than the tantrums began. As usual, my husband launched into a familiar tirade of name-calling. My "offense" was that I had disrespected him, and it was time for me to be "*dealt with*" and punished for that disrespect. During his verbal assault, he slapped me. Fortunately, we were at a traffic light. Feeling hurt, humiliated, and traumatized, I tried to exit the vehicle. The light was *red* when he slapped me, but by the time I was ready to leave, it had turned *green*. Instead of allowing me to exit safely, my husband began to drive away. In a desperate attempt to avoid being dragged along, I quickly removed my winter coat to facilitate my escape. I ran for my life, but my husband did not stop. He ran over my coat and continued on to church without me.

It had snowed all day, and with the temperature below freezing, I realized I needed to go back for my coat to avoid catching a cold, as I was only wearing sweatshirts and pants. While the coat would help keep me warm, I was still at risk for frostbite since I wasn't wearing gloves. I hurried to the nearest gas station and called my children to come and take me home. My husband stayed at Bible Study for an hour and didn't attempt to search for me before returning home. *This raised a troubling question: "Did he expect me to freeze to death and not be held accountable for his* actions?" While I couldn't answer that, his behavior was unexpected and unbecoming of a man who had promised to love and cherish me. Despite the harshness of that evening, I didn't report him to the police or leave him. Yet, it became clear that I was in deeper trouble than I had realized. That night, I felt lost and unsure of how to navigate a situation that highlighted the dangerous reality of my marriage. Unfortunately, this is a common struggle for many women in abusive relationships; they often don't know what to do or how to start over.

There was no doubt that my husband's treatment of me that evening was cruel. I was familiar with his inflated sense of self-importance and his frequent emotional manipulation, using guilt and anger to control me. He often talked down to me, called me names, belittled my achievements, and made me feel inferior. However, his behavior that night—leaving me in the cold—was a striking display of empathy deficit that I had never witnessed before. To anyone reading this, it's important to recognize that while people can sometimes act cruelly, abusers often exhibit this behavior repeatedly over time. If you are dealing with an abusive partner who is being cruel, prioritize your self-preservation and self-care, and take decisive action. Please, don't be like me.

Every abusive relationship contains fleeting moments of joy and laughter, where the abuser unexpectedly shows kindness, making everyone feel loved. I experienced my own "joyful" moments that gave me hope for a better future. However, there was always an ulterior motive behind any kindness, and these moments never lasted long. My husband had the capacity for niceness, and I often observed him being pleasant to outsiders—a common trait among abusers. His gestures were purely self-serving, as an abuser derives no genuine pleasure from positively impacting others' lives.

At times, he was nice simply to put on a show or because others were present, seizing the opportunity for a public displays of *affection (PDA).* This could occur in church, at parties, or when we hosted guests. During these moments, my husband would behave impeccably, even appearing as a lovebird. He would hug and kiss me in public, prompting envy from onlookers. Yet, it was all a facade, merely an attempt to portray himself as the ideal husband and us as the picture-perfect couple.

Unfortunately, I initially approached this exhausting situation with patience, influenced by my cultural background. I was taught that a woman must have *"aforiti,"* the Yorùbá word for perseverance, and I did my best to endure. However, there is a limit to human endurance. I now understand the importance of self-preservation, recognizing the need to define what is acceptable and intolerable. We must set clear boundaries, confidently determine what we can accept, and insist on receiving the same respect we offer as devoted wives.

The first part of Malachi 2:16 states, *"For the Lord God of Israel says that He hates divorce..."* This message was passionately conveyed in the church, and as a minister of the gospel, I counseled women accordingly. However, the Amplified Bible clarifies that God also hates something else in that verse: *"For I hate divorce," says the Lord, the God of Israel, "and him who covers his garment with wrong and violence," says the Lord of hosts. "Therefore, keep watch on your spirit, so that you do not deal treacherously with your wife."* Unfortunately, many Christians focus solely on God's hatred for divorce, ignoring the latter part of the scripture that addresses violence, treachery, and mistreatment of spouses.

God cannot be deceived, nor can the truth be hidden from Him through any pretense. Even if a man conceals his misdeeds by exercising cruelty at home rather than in public, God sees through the facade. Abusers undermine the sanctity of marriage by terrorizing their wives in private while projecting an image of being model husbands to outsiders. Regrettably, the desire to stay married and maintain a positive marital image often takes precedence over reason, allowing abuse to continue rather than curtailing it. This was true for me, as it is for many other women.

Chapter Eight

THE LONG-SUFFERING BREADWINNER

"A woman is like a tea bag. You never know how strong she is until she gets in hot water."

- ELEANOR ROOSEVELT

Early in our marriage, we lived on a tight budget, which compelled me to start a business. This was how God introduced me to cake making, an endeavor that proved quite profitable. As the *helper* I was called to be, I was happy to support my husband. However, when he was unable to earn an income from his legal practice in Nigeria, I became the primary breadwinner. This dramatic shift in traditional roles required me to work exceptionally hard to provide for our family.

While it is not entirely new in Nigeria for women to support their families, the role of breadwinner has historically belonged to men. However, as more women gain education and employment, and as some men face job loss or underemployment, traditional breadwinning roles are increasingly challenged and sometimes reversed, leading to more women becoming the primary earners in their households.

Even before my wedding, the term "helper" in Genesis 2:18 has held special significance for *me: "And the Lord God said, 'It is not good that man should be alone; I will make him a helper comparable to him.'"* I have always believed that this scripture speaks to the essence of what God intended for marriage. While we are all called to support one another, the Bible particularly emphasizes this responsibility for wives. Although a man's help may take many forms, the most significant source of that support is his wife. As a helper to my husband, I viewed my role as sharing life's responsibilities, as mutually agreed upon with him, and providing both physical and spiritual support. Ultimately, I believed my husband would need my help to maintain balance in our marriage, and I committed to offering him my unwavering support.

When we arrived in the United States, my husband found work, but it was insufficient. He chose contract-based employment, which lasted only a few months at a time. Once he became a minister, he stopped working altogether, unlike many of his peers who managed to balance full-time jobs with ministry work. This decision plunged us into financial hardship, forcing me to take two jobs to help us survive day by day. At least we were able to pay our bills, especially with substantial financial support from my late parents.

Having been raised by a strong, hardworking mother, I learned the value of hard work and was not afraid to face challenges. With a family to support and my husband's income often meager or nonexistent, I had little choice but to roll up my sleeves and dedicate myself to my family's well-being. I felt that the term "service" accurately described the sacrifices I was making for them at that time. My husband had promised to work hard to provide for us, but he did not follow through, even after a friend advised him to seek employment. He developed an unfortunate habit of quitting jobs impulsively, acting on his own whims. No matter how much I expressed my concerns about his irresponsible attitude toward work, especially given our precarious financial situation, it made no difference to him.

I was fortunate to receive numerous perks and bonuses at my job, which helped stabilize our finances. However, we still struggled to afford simple luxuries like going to the movies, dining out, or taking the occasional vacation. Being the family breadwinner was challenging enough without the added burden of managing household chores such as cooking, cleaning, and other responsibilities. Nevertheless, I managed it all with joy and without complaint. Given my efforts to improve our difficult financial situation, one might have expected some appreciation and kindness from my husband, but the reality was quite the opposite. He remained as harsh as ever, even more so than he had been in Nigeria. To make matters worse, he spent the money I worked so hard for in a reckless manner, ignoring the family's needs. Consequently, I had to compensate for any shortfall by working extra hours and taking cake orders, even when it was inconvenient. Eventually, the cake business, which had been financially beneficial for us both in Nigeria and the United States, became a contentious issue, and he tried to shut it down. I stood my ground, having become wise enough to set boundaries he could not cross. In any case, he could only express his frustration through rants.

My husband was relentless in his quest for control, always finding ways to remind me that he was in charge, despite my role as the family's provider. I recall an incident regarding new drapery for our home. We had agreed on the design before I left for work that morning. However, when I returned in the evening, I was surprised to find that the drapery had been installed in a manner completely opposite to our agreement. When I asked him why he changed it, he simply stated that he had decided to *"switch things up."* I tried to express my displeasure, but his response was to question whether he couldn't have a say in how the drapery was installed just because I was paying for it. I quickly realized that his *decision to "switch things up"* was a way to assert his dominance, so I chose to remain silent and let the matter drop.

Those were the types of behaviors I had to endure from the harsh and unkind man I married. I not only dreaded being around him, but I also learned to choose my battles wisely, responding only when it was absolutely necessary. Undoubtedly, a man's treatment of others, especially when he is angry, speaks louder than anything else he does. No matter how much he quotes scripture to cloak himself *in righteousness,* the way he treats others is a true measure of his spirituality and his relationship with God. Matthew 7:15-16 *states, "Beware of false prophets, who come to you in sheep's clothing, but inwardly they are ravenous wolves. You will know them by their fruits. Do men gather grapes from thornbushes or figs from thistles?"* This means that while a man may profess to know God, it is by their fruits that we will truly understand who they are.

Dear Reader, if your story resembles mine in any way, I urge you to learn from my experiences and to dare to approach things differently than I did. The best way to begin is to talk to someone about what you are going through. I encourage you to speak up and refuse to be intimidated.

Chapter Nine

MASTER OF TRIANGULATION

"...Narcissists like to manufacture love triangles and bring in the opinions of others to validate their point of view."

- SHAHIDA ARABI

My husband was a master of triangulation. Unfortunately, I didn't understand what triangulation was until I began researching abuse, narcissism, and personality disorders. I learned that triangulation is a powerful tool in the hands of an abuser. It occurs when a toxic or manipulative person, often with significant narcissistic traits, introduces a third person into their relationship to create conflict between them and their partner. The abuser's ultimate goal is to sow discord so they can *divide and conquer,* control the narrative, and isolate their partner from friends and support systems. The key phrase here is *"divide and* conquer," which is a strategy that enables a person to maintain power by ensuring that those under their influence disagree and fight each other, preventing them from uniting against the abuser. The abuser understands that while there is strength in unity, division leads to control. In keeping with the dreadful conduct typical of an abuser, "divide and conquer" is a strategy of the cunning and a weapon of the weak.

Darius Cikanavicius, a certified mental health coach with extensive research on narcissism, explains that individuals who triangulate view others as objects that reflect or extend themselves, existing solely to protect their ego. Until I started researching abuse and narcissism, I was unaware of triangulation and that I was being subjected to it. Once I understood the concept, I realized that my husband had been triangulating for a long time, and I quickly recognized the classic dynamics of triangulation in my own life. I was the victim—ashamed, helpless, hopeless, and powerless—while my husband played the *role of the authority* figure—superior, controlling, and oppressive. The third parties in this scenario were friends he had skillfully convinced that I was the source of any problems in our marriage.

My research revealed that abusers typically target your friends and anyone who admires you. They become jealous of the affection and admiration you receive, striving to appropriate it for themselves. I encountered numerous examples of this in my marriage, particularly a memorable incident at a conference where we met a couple who were both pastors. The wife gifted me a wallet, but my husband reacted with anger, questioning why I was the recipient of a gift when he was the pastor, and I was "just his wife." *Shouldn't a husband celebrate his wife's recognition and appreciate the giver?* That is the expected behavior of normal people. However, abusive individuals can only celebrate themselves. I was taken aback by my husband's intense anger and jealousy, and the drive home was filled with tension and resentment.

Another indication of his need for attention was his tendency to dominate conversations, often portraying himself as more knowledgeable than I was about the topic at hand. He craved applause whenever possible, and if he did not receive it, it became a sore point for him, driving him to seek validation by any means necessary.

Triangulation is a tactic used by abusers to manipulate your friends into changing their perceptions of you, ultimately turning them against you. This process is often so subtle and stealthy that it goes almost unnoticed. In my experience, my husband would initiate triangulation by inviting a mutual friend to mediate our issues, ostensibly to help resolve our conflicts. At the time, I thought nothing of these interventions, not realizing what I was truly facing until much later. Initially, he would speak positively about me to these friends, who were usually mine since he did not have any friends of his own.

Once he gained their trust, he would move on to the next stage of his carefully orchestrated scheme. That's when the lies would start. He would say things *like, "I think you should know this about my wife. She is very disrespectful to me. I know you think she's a great wife, but America has changed her; she is no longer the person you knew years ago."* After convincing them that I wasn't the virtuous person they believed me to be—or at least not the good wife I was supposed to be—they tended to believe him, simply because he was my husband. As a result, they began to avoid me, branding me as "bad company."

I remember a friend telling me I had become "modernized," but this statement didn't make sense until some of my other friends began sharing what my husband had been saying about me. I was taken aback by the level of treachery he had sunk to, and it left me grappling with a whirlwind of emotions. I felt humiliated and struggled to decide whether to go on the *defensive. Should I try to correct the false impression he had* created? I attempted to, but the damage was already done. Unfortunately, this is often the goal of an abuser, who seeks to isolate you from your support system.

I lost friends because of triangulation, yet I am grateful that I did not lose my faith. I understood that, despite my husband's misrepresentation of God, he did not die for me. Jesus, the *One* who loved me unconditionally and sacrificed Himself for me, is the reason I remain steadfast. My husband may have been a skilled preacher, but he chose not to submit to the authority of the Word of God and did not live by the example he preached. As incredulous as this narrative may seem to some, it was my reality.

Chapter Ten

THE CHURCH IS NOT AN IMPARTIAL ARBITER

"More men and women of God must learn and then speak, preach, and teach the truth about domestic violence, how widespread it is, and how some Christian teachings can be twisted to condone, deny, and exacerbate it. Society and the church minimize abuse. We must speak the truth and work together to end domestic violence and sexual assault."

- THE REVEREND AL MILES, *LEAD CHAPLAIN, THE QUEEN'S MEDICAL CENTER, HONOLULU, HAWAII. AUTHOR, "DOMESTIC VIOLENCE: WHAT EVERY PASTOR NEEDS TO KNOW."*

While I have tried to keep third parties out of my narrative, it is essential to address the role of the church and its members in my story. My aim is not to humiliate anyone or discredit church leaders, but rather to illuminate the church's ignorance regarding abuse. The church is the bride of Jesus Christ, whom He protects with utmost care, passion, and jealousy; we, as His disciples, must do the same. Therefore, I want to clarify that while I do not intend to disparage the church, I feel a responsibility to help it recognize the presence of wolves among us. We must confront these threats to safeguard the interests of Christ's bride, just as He would.

Many leaders in society seek power and control over others, using various oppressive and manipulative tactics to achieve their selfish goals. Such unscrupulous individuals can be found in politics, large corporations, and even small businesses. Unfortunately, they have also infiltrated the church and the Body of Christ in significant numbers. I once heard of a church minister whose wife was the worship leader; each time he took the microphone from her after worship, he would threaten her in low, menacing tones, warning her not to disclose his abuse. I also read about a brother who murdered his wife in cold blood; although he is now incarcerated, her life was tragically lost to abuse. The story of Sister Osinachi Nwachukwu, a well-known Nigerian gospel artist who died as a direct result of violence from her husband, remains fresh in our collective memory. Sadly, we hear daily of many such instances of domestic violence ending in unnecessary fatalities, illustrating the troubling behavior of men sitting in *pews* and standing in *pulpits* in our churches today. The greater tragedy is that many of these men now hold leadership positions in the church, where they wield control and manipulation over their spouses and others within the congregation.

A good woman does not walk away from her marriage without fighting for it. However, when she becomes weary from the struggle, she may ultimately choose to leave, as I did. As believers, we recognize the scriptural mandate to protect the institution of marriage and genuinely desire to uphold it. Yet, we must also ensure that we are not inadvertently endorsing or enabling abuse within the church. We should strive to save marriages whenever possible, but when it becomes clear that a marriage has irretrievably broken down and that abuse is the undeniable cause of discord, we must support the woman in taking her next steps, whatever they may be.

I want to emphasize that my intention in discussing the church's role in my story is to raise awareness about this issue and to assist women like me who may not know how to escape their abusive situations. While it is an undeniable truth that God can and will deliver His daughters, we must also take on the responsibility of being our sisters' keepers in their times of need. If the church had been more aware of the evil within, perhaps Sister Osinachi would still be alive today.

Unfortunately, she is not. Nevertheless, we can focus on helping others who are still suffering under the cruelty of their husbands.

In my situation, the brethren were not particularly supportive. They often vilified me, using scripture as a means to justify my husband's abuse. There was considerable emotional and spiritual manipulation from the church community, with comments like, "*What did you do to provoke him?*" implying that my lack of submission was the root of the abuse. The church views marriage as a lifelong commitment, expecting nothing less than permanence. Consequently, the common refrain from pastors and congregants was that God hates divorce, insisting that I uphold my vow of "*for better or* worse," even when I was at my breaking point. One pastor told me that, as a pastor, he could not support my decision to leave, even in light of my deteriorating health, insisting that I should continue to fast and pray until my husband changed. Eventually, I reached a point where I could no longer fast. To this day, I remain puzzled as to why my husband was not encouraged to fast and pray for his own change.

In my view, such counsel reflects a patriarchal mindset, particularly evident in Nigerian society. Women are expected to shoulder all responsibilities while men, as the glorified "*Lords of the Manor,*" sit back and enjoy the fruits of their labor. I often found this attitude appalling within the church and wondered if these brothers and sisters would feel differently if I were their sister or daughter. Some church members would engage in conversations with my husband when I was absent, allowing him to manipulate the narrative through triangulation. As a result, I became the villain while he assumed the role of the victim. Eventually, I realized it was better to be the villain in his story than to risk my life or well-being trying to preserve a non-existent marriage.

One of the greatest challenges faced by abused women is the struggle to be heard; many feel their voices go unnoticed. The second challenge is convincing others of the mistreatment they endure, particularly because of the favorable image their abuser projects to the world. Throughout my marriage, most church members either ignored my pleas or chose not to believe me. Even those who did listen were often more concerned about the church's reputation than my well-being, as I became the sacrificial lamb for the sake of its integrity. A pastor even texted me, saying, *"You can both yield to God's way of resolution and not allow the enemy to destroy many lives. The window of opportunity is* short." *I questioned, "What is God's way of resolution in light of 2 Timothy 3:1-5, which advises turning away from individuals with the characteristics described in those verses?"* The full text of 2 Timothy 3:1-5 (NKJV) *states, "But know this, that in the last days perilous times will come. For men will be lovers of themselves, lovers of money, boasters, proud, blasphemers, disobedient to parents, unthankful, unholy, unloving, unforgiving, slanderers, without self-control, brutal, despisers of good, traitors, headstrong, haughty, lovers of pleasure rather than lovers of God, having a form of godliness but denying its power. And from such people turn away!"*

To the pastor who sent me that text, saving the lives of others was more important than saving my own. For many church leaders, *"others"* were all they cared about, but I refused to be sacrificed on the altar of ministry. The church is the bride of Jesus Christ, and since He already died for her, no one should be expected to lay down their life for the stability of a church or ministry. Unfortunately, this truth and its significance seemed lost on everyone but me. Even after I separated from my husband, who launched a smear campaign against me, I was still urged to return solely because God supposedly hates divorce. However, I believed our God did not want me to continue suffering, so I refused to go back.

Some of the brethren were more interested in the gossip surrounding my situation than in the pain I was enduring, turning me into a topic for malicious gossip. When it was all said and done, not one righteous man stood up to my husband to confront his despicable behavior. Instead of addressing the issue, they adopted a misguided *stance of diplomacy,* ostensibly to avoid upsetting him, but they missed the point: he was already upset with me and always had been. A few brave friends attempted to ask my husband some difficult questions, and once they uncovered the truth, he turned against them, seeing them as enemies and cutting them off.

Churches must confront certain social issues, and spousal abuse is one of the most misunderstood and mismanaged by church leaders. A significant number of women do not view their pastors as sources of help when they are victims of abuse. Many pastors tell abused women to be more submissive to their abusive husbands or suggest that they stay and trust God. These pastors teach that the Bible requires wives to submit, even to abusive husbands. Sadly, submission does not stop abuse; it often intensifies it by giving the abusive husband a greater sense of power and allowing him to escape painful consequences for his actions. It is disheartening that church leaders do not condemn abuse from the pulpit. While some pastors make unhelpful statements in response to abuse, they often remain silent about what truly needs to be said: God hates abuse, and it is sinful and unacceptable.

A few church leaders recognized that my husband mistreated me and acknowledged that my health, safety, and well-being were more important than ministry. I am genuinely grateful to those individuals. Throughout my marriage, I frequently received counsel urging me to *"continue loving my husband, pray for him, provide him with more food and sex—these are the keys to a man's heart—and stop fabricating issues because 'he can't be that bad.'"* Believe me when I say that I *prayed* intensely. I loved, fasted, and *prayed* in response to their advice, but my efforts were in vain. You will understand why when you learn about the nature of abusive spouses.

After separating from my husband, he spread various falsehoods about me, yet I was still advised to return to him. Common phrases used to persuade me included, *"You've been with him too long to leave now," "You can't leave; he's your project,"* and *"What about the ministry?"* They failed to grasp that my husband cared nothing for the ministry or the church members; all he valued was his image. Even though he was indifferent to the damage done to maintain his carefully crafted facade, I believe I contributed to that harm by not speaking out, and it's time to correct that.

To my dear sister, reading this book, understand that if you were to die at the hands of an abusive husband, life would continue, and he would likely marry again. A man has just taken a fourth wife after leaving three previous ones, struggling to rebuild their lives. It is crucial to free yourself from this toxic environment while you still can and start anew, even if that means beginning from scratch. I know that the primary concern of an abuse victim is, *"Where and how do I begin to rebuild my life?"* However, my sister, I assure you that with a strong support system, everything will ultimately work out for the best. You must take that step now; tomorrow may be too late.

Chapter Eleven

A LITANY OF PSYCHOSOMATIC AILMENTS

"Healing takes courage, and we all have courage, even if we have to dig a little to find it."

-TORI AMOS

Although I later confided in a few pastors about my situation, only three people in my life knew the full truth about my marriage. Unfortunately, there was little they could do to help; their support was limited to praying for me and with me. My girlfriend in the United Kingdom confronted my husband about his troubling behavior, but he dismissed her concerns with the absurd accusation that she wanted me to leave him. He attempted to manipulate another friend into taking his side, but she quickly saw through his deceit and refused to believe his stories, leading him to cut her off as well.

My friends became my pillars of support, continuously praying for my strength and, specifically, for a change of heart in my husband. I also had a spiritual mentor who fasted and prayed alongside me for a transformation in my marriage. Despite our collective hope, the situation only worsened. Our pastor friend, whose wife was my high school classmate, visited multiple times to reason with my husband, but his efforts were fruitless. Many of the third parties my husband contacted eventually grew weary of hearing the same narrative and withdrew their support, leaving me to navigate my struggles alone while advising me to "just be patient."

In my quest for relief from my marital troubles, I joined every prayer group I could find, desperate for answers and an end to the pain and trauma. Yet, nothing changed; my husband remained unwilling to alter his behavior, perpetuating the cycle of abuse. The stress took a toll on my body, and I realized I was not only losing my mind but also my sense of self. When I got married, I was a vibrant and beautiful woman, but by the time I left my husband, I felt like a mere shadow of my former self. I was constantly told there was nothing beautiful about me, and soon I began to believe it. It wasn't until after I had left him that I recognized, despite the passing years, I am still beautiful. The impact on my mental health was profound, and there were moments when I wandered the streets lost in chaotic thoughts, feeling like a madwoman.

I often found myself driving around aimlessly, fearful of returning home, uncertain of what awaited me. On many of those days, I faced accusations of infidelity, which I had come to expect. The pain from the sciatic nerve in my right leg, a result of a fall while clearing snow, was often excruciating, and I quickly became reliant on pain medications. The stress and trauma caused me to lose my appetite, and when I did feel hungry, I turned to comfort foods, with plantain being my top choice. It had always been my favorite, and its ease of preparation made it my go-to meal. I also tolerated fruits and vegetables, consuming them in large quantities, but my health continued to decline rapidly.

In response to my deteriorating health, my doctor advised a dietary change, and I eventually began making healthier food choices. However, my limited intake left me very thin, nearly frail, and constantly fatigued. Alongside my weight loss, I struggled with insomnia and unexplained joint pain, attributed to inflammation, which is often the root of many ailments. After years of trauma and living in constant fear, I developed anxiety and panic attacks. Much later in my marriage, I also began experiencing high blood pressure. My blood sugar levels spiraled out of control, and my doctor diagnosed my persistent joint pain as arthritis, despite my being under fifty at the time.

I experienced persistent back pain and a bulge at the back of my neck that wouldn't go away, despite weekly visits to a chiropractor. It was only through research that I learned the bulge was a result of the abuse and toxicity I had endured. As I studied the effects of abuse and stress, I discovered that the body remains in a constant state of fight or flight, which causes the muscles in the neck and shoulders to tighten, literally "bunching" up until a bulge forms at the back of the neck. Thankfully, that bulge has disappeared as I began my healing journey, and I am truly grateful to God for the new direction my life has taken.

During this time, I also dealt with hair loss, known as alopecia, and suffered from lower back pain. At some point—though I can't pinpoint exactly when—I lost my sense of smell. I loved wearing perfumes and would apply them generously, yet I couldn't perceive their scent. The only way I knew I smelled good was when friends or colleagues complimented me on whichever fragrance I was wearing. The first time I detected my perfume again after many years was about six months after my husband and I separated, marking a significant moment in my healing process.

Throughout my marriage, I prayed fervently for healing, but it eluded me. This wasn't because God didn't want to heal me; rather, I couldn't heal while remaining in a toxic environment. It became evident that I couldn't recover in the space that had caused my suffering, as my wounds needed the freedom to breathe and regenerate. Stress had become a way of life for me, leading to the development of coping mechanisms that hindered my healing. LaTarsha Holden, in her book *It's Okay to Be a Mess*, accurately describes women like me, who are expected to *"work 40-50 hours a week, not be tired, keep a tidy house, tend to the children, support their husbands, and silently suffer* burnout." I was that woman—her words resonated with me deeply. The burnout I experienced manifested in various ailments. According to Danish Bashir, the effects of narcissistic abuse can show up in the body as insomnia, diabetes, chronic fatigue, lack of concentration, hormonal imbalances, tension, high blood pressure, and memory problems, among other issues.

Bessel van der Kolk, in his book *The Body Keeps the Score*, explains that traumatized individuals secrete large amounts of stress hormones and experience increased adrenaline levels, which can severely impact their long-term health and nervous system. He highlights that consistently elevated stress hormones can lead to memory and attention issues. Dr. Nicole LePera also asserts that trauma is stored in the body, noting that in toxic environments, cortisol levels spike, causing inflammation as the body attempts to combat an emotional infection. However, she suggests that many symptoms can dissipate when the abused individual finds themselves in healthier surroundings. I can personally attest to this, as my own experience reflects that my body *truly "kept the* score." The persistent emotional stress I endured manifested in various physical ailments.

Despite feeling deeply sad and frustrated by my situation, I was at a loss for how to achieve freedom. I believed that fasting and prayer would provide the answers—a common mistake among many believers. Instead of speaking out in the right contexts, we often shrink back in fear, enabling our own abuse to continue. After years of suffering and confusion, a friend, who was also a survivor of narcissistic abuse, encouraged me to research the topics of abuse and narcissism. Through this research, I discovered that the numerous ailments I experienced were rooted in the stress of the abuse and toxicity I had been facing.

CHAPTER TWELVE
THE NARCISSIST

"Relationships with narcissists are held in place by the hope of a 'someday better,' with little evidence to support it will ever arrive."

- DR. RAMANI

Narcissism has become a prevalent theme in our society. While I do not believe that every abuser is a narcissist, I address the topic in this chapter to assist at least one person married to one. Although narcissism has existed for a long time, social media has recently brought it into the contemporary spotlight. The abundance of information available online may lead one to conclude that it has become a pandemic. However, I contend that, despite its epidemic nature, no one is born a narcissist. As recorded in Genesis 1:30, everything God created was very good. Humanity was made in God's image, and nothing about God embodies evil or narcissism.

Dr. Cory Newman, a psychology professor at the University of Pennsylvania, defines a narcissist as someone exhibiting a pervasive pattern of grandiosity, a need for admiration, and a lack of empathy. He notes that these behaviors typically emerge in early adulthood. Mac Davidson, a narcissism expert writing on *Quora*, argues that such behavior is *learned, stating, "no baby or child can conceive of what behavior they will adopt twenty years later. It is a phenomenological response to feeling unworthy and unlovable."*

Through my research, I found that children may adopt narcissistic behaviors from parents who overvalue them or who believe they are more special than others in their family or environment. This phenomenon is similar to the *"spoilt child syndrome."* The Mayo Clinic also confirms that one cause of narcissism can be found in parent-child relationships characterized by excessive adoration or disproportionate criticism that does not align with the child's experiences or achievements.

I urge parents to avoid raising children, regardless of gender, in ways that may lead them to become narcissistic adults. Children who are not taught to apologize for their wrongdoing, to be empathetic, and who are encouraged to feel exaggerated importance in relation to their siblings or adults in the home are likely to develop into selfish, narcissistic adults if left unchecked.

It is important to recognize that while narcissists can be male or female, the underlying issues are often the same for both.

Thanks to a friend's suggestion, I began my research on this topic and was astonished to uncover the true nature of narcissism.

WHAT YOU SEE IS NOT WHAT YOU GET

The first thing I learned about narcissists is that they are not who they claim to be. Initially, they present themselves as confident, charming, caring, and kind, showcasing many positive traits. However, what people often fail to see right away is that they are bullies who lack empathy, crave social attention, have no genuine friends or accountability partners, are pathological liars, and harbor intense jealousy of others. In my over five years of exhaustive research into narcissism, I have identified several key characteristics:

- Narcissists are highly sensitive individuals who exhibit a sense of entitlement, a desire to control others, a lack of empathy, manipulative behavior, and resistance to criticism. They take any criticism as a personal affront and are unlikely to forgive those who challenge them.

- They believe they are special and unique, expecting everyone to treat them accordingly. Anyone who does not comply is seen as an enemy or of no value, warranting punishment through persistent attempts at revenge.
- Narcissists are unforgiving, and their remarkable memory reinforces this trait. They do not forget or forgive wrongs. Additionally, anything you share with them on a personal level will likely be remembered and used against you later.
- They feel entitled to the best in life, believing it is their right, yet they also think they shouldn't have to work for what they want. This leads them to constantly seek what is *known as "narcissistic supply."*
- Anyone who challenges them, especially those who impede their supply, can expect aggression and narcissistic rage.
- They possess a fragile sense of self that drives them to seek validation and demand respect, even when it is unearned.
- Narcissists are self-absorbed and often dominate conversations, talking over others to assert their superiority. They also strive to have the last word.

- Their ego compels them to outshine others; if they cannot do so, they resort to devaluing those around them to boost their own self-esteem.
- They have a deep-seated need for attention, which energizes them, although only those close to them recognize this underlying desire.
- They project an inflated sense of intelligence, often using elaborate language to create an impression of superiority.
- Ultimately, the narcissist idolizes themselves. Rather than encouraging you to worship a higher power, they demand your admiration and seek to be the center of your attention.
- They believe they are always right and, due to their lack of self-awareness and inability to reflect, can never perceive themselves as being wrong. They employ *blame shifting* to evade accountability.
- A defining characteristic of narcissists is their constant criticism and the demeaning or devaluing of others.
- The "Christian" narcissist manipulates scripture for personal gain, pretending to adhere to its teachings while actually disregarding them.

- They view scripture as a weapon for judging others, yet consider themselves too superior to be judged. Anyone who attempts to correct them becomes an enemy, subject to an enduring hatred.
- Believing themselves superior, the "Christian" narcissist uses *Ephesians 5:22, "Wives, submit to your own husbands, as to the Lord,"* to justify unquestionable control over their spouse.
- The "Christian" narcissist boasts about their own achievements and those of their children as if they were their own. They often seek to completely subjugate their children to their will by citing *Exodus 20:12, "Honor your father and your mother, that your days may be long upon the land which the Lord your God is giving you."*
- It takes very little to provoke a narcissist, leading to a constant state of rage, which they use as a tool to instill fear in their victims, who are always walking on eggshells.
- Their notion of forgiveness involves expecting acceptance of their insincere apologies, while continuing their harmful behaviors.
- They project their own actions onto their victims, accusing them of the very behaviors they exhibit.

- They seek connections with others solely for personal gain. If you are eager for any kind of relationship, you may find yourself carrying the burden for both parties.
- They marry to create the facade of a good husband and family man, but behind closed doors, they are monstrous to the very people they use to maintain that image, objectifying them to serve their purposes.
- They choose strong, hardworking, and supportive partners but ultimately come to resent them for the very qualities that attracted them initially.
- They select kind, compassionate, and loyal individuals as spouses, only to gradually destroy them through relentless criticism and devaluation.
- They exploit those around them, especially those closest to them, whether through emotional, financial, or social means.
- They are master manipulators who effectively isolate their victims from friends, family, and support networks that could help them escape.
- They cannot achieve their desires if their true nature is exposed, so they feign kindness and understanding.

- They have everything to gain by tarnishing their spouse's reputation, so they manipulate situations to protect their own image and discredit their partner.
- When you leave a narcissist, they may pretend to want you back and tell others the same. However, each time you return, you signal your willingness to tolerate their harmful behavior.
- As they age, they desperately strive to maintain a façade of youth and control, often resorting to tactics like dyeing their hair and mustache.
- To convince themselves of their continued youth and virility, they reminisce about their past achievements, boasting to anyone who will listen in an attempt to impress.
- Their temper tantrums persist throughout their lives, yet they portray themselves as victims, claiming they sacrificed their dreams for others without receiving appreciation.
- With age, they often become increasingly vindictive, resentful, and bitter, particularly towards their spouse.
- Some narcissists harbor misogynistic views, which typically stem from early life trauma inflicted by a trusted female figure.

UNDERSTANDING THE COMMUNICATION STYLE OF THE NARCISSIST

Despite their claims of love for others, the only person a narcissist truly cares about is themselves and their image. The truth lies in their words, making it crucial to discern the underlying meanings behind their communication.

- *When they say "I love you," it means "I want to control you at all costs."*
- *When they say "You are ugly, and nobody else can marry you," it means "You are beautiful, and I fear losing you to someone else."*
- *When they say "You are of no value," it means "I know I am not worthy of you, so I will devalue you."*
- *When they accuse you of cheating, it means "I am cheating; you just don't know it."*
- *When they say "I want you back," it means "I need you back because I have run out of emotional supply."*
- *When they claim "Everybody hates you and speaks ill of you," it means "I have been conducting a smear campaign against you."*

This is not an exhaustive list, and if you want to learn more—especially if you suspect you're in a relationship with a narcissist—there are numerous online resources available. After gathering the information mentioned above, I found myself in a daze. I realized that if I had known what I do now ten years ago, I would likely have made different choices. It took me over five years to compile this knowledge, but I finally understood what I was facing. Although it was overwhelming and brought me to tears, I began establishing boundaries to protect my well-being and sanity. As Jim Rohn said, *"we must suffer one of two things: the pain of discipline or the pain of regret or disappointment."* For me, it was the latter. I carried many regrets and disappointments from years gone by, and I knew there was no way to undo the past.

The years of pain and trauma had taken a toll on me, and I was ready to break the cycle of destruction. However, I was uncertain about the right course of action. I had already left the relationship twice, and each time I returned, conditions worsened, making it clear that my return indicated acceptance of the harmful behavior. I grappled with the question: *Should I leave or stay?* Leslie Vernick, in her book *The Emotionally Destructive Marriage*, advises that every woman in an abusive marriage must choose wisely. She emphasized that anyone who decides to stay should do so consciously, and anyone who chooses to leave must do so with intention. I knew I had to determine the best step forward for my situation. Fortunately, I eventually arrived at the right decision.

CHAPTER THIRTEEN
AT A CROSSROADS

"When you are the only one in your marriage caring, repenting, being respectful and honest, sacrificing, and working toward being a better spouse, you are a godly wife, but you don't have a healthy or biblical marriage."

- LESLIE VERNICK, IN *THE EMOTIONALLY DESTRUCTIVE MARRIAGE: HOW TO FIND YOUR VOICE AND RECLAIM YOUR HOPE*

By the time you reach this chapter, you may be questioning why I stayed in my difficult marriage for so long. You might feel righteous anger at my inability to speak up for myself, and that reaction is completely understandable. I felt that anger too. I was frustrated with myself for remaining loyal to a man who treated me poorly and for losing sight of who I was. I had left the marriage twice, but each return only worsened the situation, which is a common outcome when dealing with a narcissist.

The second time I left, my husband wrote me a letter apologizing for years of abuse and promising to change. However, when I returned, his promised transformation was fleeting, and my circumstances became even more dire. In her book, *The Emotionally Destructive Marriage*, Leslie Vernick highlights that many women persist in trying to please their husbands because they believe it aligns with God's expectations. Yet, she also warns that submitting to this "god" leads to being governed by fear rather than guided by God's love. This description resonates not only with my experience but also with many women who find themselves under the control of an abusive partner.

Once I understood the reality of my situation, everything began to make sense. With an abuser, you are not a partner but a servant. Furthermore, you often become a single mother, left to raise your children alone. The abuser prioritizes their own needs above all else, relegating your needs to the bottom of the list. The loneliness you endure is indescribable, especially when their phone, rather than their spouse, becomes their constant companion. They are often more accessible to strangers than to their family and more interested in impressing others than in caring for those at home.

Dr. Hawkins, founder and director of the *Marriage Recovery Center*, explains that narcissism is characterized by pride and self-centeredness. It embodies sin and reflects a broken attachment to God and others. My shocking discoveries suddenly clarified many past experiences: the name-calling, devaluing, demeaning behavior, false accusations of adultery, and the misuse of scripture to silence me. I had always wondered why my husband could counsel other couples using scripture yet failed to apply those principles in our own home, but now I understood.

However, recognizing the truth about my situation did not prevent my overwhelming feelings of despair and the tears that flowed freely. I cried extensively, deeply wounded, damaged, and traumatized. Though I had lived in a hopeful dreamland for too long, I had finally awakened to the harsh reality of my life and marital dysfunction. I recalled the red flags I had ignored and the excuses I had made for my husband. I also remembered my parents' warnings early in my marriage, which I dismissed because they were not believers, while my husband and I were. I had been naïve and trusting, and even though my husband sometimes called me a fool, I finally recognized how right he was about my foolishness over the years.

Where would I begin to piece together my shattered hopes and dreams? I had no clear path forward, but I was determined not to abandon my faith. I often recalled the divine encounter that brought me to the Lord, using it as a reminder that He was with me. Clinging to this hope, I cried out to God for deliverance, much like He had freed the children of Israel from Pharaoh's grasp. I once heard Bishop T.D. Jakes say, *"tears are a gift from God to ventilate the soul when you have been in pain,"* and so I allowed my tears to flow. I wept until my eyes hurt, knowing there was no turning back the hands of time.

Despite all I had uncovered during my research, I did not leave immediately, as every resource warned about the need for caution. I found myself at a crossroads, uncertain of my next step, but I began to establish boundaries. Implementing these boundaries led to accusations of selfishness, yet I had been selfless for too long and no longer cared about others' opinions. Still, I weighed my options carefully and spent considerable time in prayer, hoping that clarity would come in due time. However, it felt like an eternity before I gained any insight. The trauma I had experienced only added to my confusion, but my research had made it clear that leaving came with serious implications—just as staying did. Ultimately, I realized I had to make a decision.

In her book, *The Emotionally Destructive Marriage*, Leslie Vernick discusses the characters Nabal and Abigail. She portrays Nabal as a destructive figure—harsh, indifferent, selfish, hotheaded, and hardhearted—while highlighting Abigail's commitment to being God-centered rather than husband-centered or self-centered. Drawing wisdom from Vernick's insights, I recognized it was time to shift from being husband-centered to God-centered. The Lord reminded me of the persecution I faced when I first got saved; despite that challenging period, I had remained steadfast in my faith. He assured me that, in my current situation, I was not only as strong as ever but stronger than I realized, and that I would be okay. Admittedly, I was unsure of what *"I would be fine"* meant, but I was willing to wait and see how God would work this time. I had hidden my pain for far too long, and while I couldn't change the past, I was certain of one thing: I could start anew and create a better future, free from pain and marital dysfunction. The pressing question was, *"How would I go about my liberation?"*

Despite the loneliness they experience in their dysfunctional marriages, many women controlled by their abusers hesitate to leave out of fear of being alone and starting over—especially since they have lost many friends due to triangulation. Let us support our sisters by being vigilant and asking questions when things seem off. I have a word of advice for believers in the church: your pastor's wife may be in pain and in need of care herself. Please check in on her and ensure she is alright. More often than not, she carries burdens far greater than you might imagine.

Chapter Fourteen

A WINDOW OF OPPORTUNITY

"........we all have that one moment. A moment when you see clearly how your life might change – the only decision you have to make is if you're going to pay attention to the fact that it's there."

- **TUNDE OYENEYIN, IN "*SPEAK - FIND YOUR VOICE, TRUST YOUR GUT, AND GET FROM WHERE YOU ARE TO WHERE YOU WANT TO BE.*"**

As a young woman, I often heard the saying, *"God works in miraculous ways, His wonders to perform."* These words begin the Christian *hymn, "God Moves in a Mysterious Way,"* written in 1773 by the 18th-century English poet William Cowper. Originally titled *"Light Shining Out of Darkness,"* it was penned after Cowper's attempted suicide following a period of deep depression and anguish. From his profound suffering emerged this emotive poetry, which later inspired music. The hymn begins:

God moves in a mysterious way,

_His wonders to perform;
He plants His footsteps in the sea,
And rides upon the storm.

Deep in unfathomable mines,
Of never failing skill;
He treasures up His bright designs,
And works His sovereign will.

Ye fearful saints fresh courage take,
The clouds ye so much dread;
Are big with mercy, and shall break,
In blessings on your head.

Judge not the Lord by feeble sense,
But trust Him for His grace;
Behind a frowning providence,
He hides a smiling face.

His purposes will ripen fast,
Unfolding every hour;
The bud may have a bitter taste,
But sweet will be the flower.

Blind unbelief is sure to err,
And scan His work in vain;
God is His own interpreter,
*And He will make it plain.*_

The first line of the hymn has evolved into the well-known proverb, *"God moves in mysterious ways"* or *"The Lord moves in miraculous ways."* It was with the spirit of those words that God, in His infinite wisdom and boundless mercy, chose to perform a great miracle, freeing me from the shackles of a dysfunctional marriage. Anyone who finds solace in those words can also draw strength from Romans 8:35-39: *"Who shall separate us from the love of Christ? Shall tribulation, or distress, or persecution, or famine, or nakedness, or peril, or sword? As it is written: "For Your sake we are killed all day long; we are accounted as sheep for the slaughter. "Yet in all these things we are more than conquerors through Him who loved us. For I am persuaded that neither death nor life, nor angels nor principalities nor powers, nor things present nor things to come, nor height nor depth, nor any other created thing, shall be able to separate us from the love of God which is in Christ Jesus our Lord."*

While contemplating and praying about the information I had gathered on narcissism, I decided to attend a *Christian Camp* to seek God's guidance. Upon arriving at the camp, I laid prostrate before God, akin to one in sackcloth with ashes on her head, crying out for help. After my fervent supplication, I felt assured in my spirit that God would assist me. Although I was filled with a curious excitement, I had no idea how it would happen. A few weeks later, an opportunity arose at work for much-needed on-the-job training in another state, and I shared this with my husband. He was also going on a trip, so we both set off for our respective journeys. Unfortunately, I fell ill right before my trip, making it a challenging endeavor, but God was with me. Thankfully, I had family in that state, where I stayed. Little did I know that this would be the escape route God had prepared for me.

I left for a few weeks of training with only two travel bags, fully believing I would return home. However, my husband's malicious actions unexpectedly pushed me toward my decision to leave him. Upon his return from a trip, he launched a smear campaign typical of an abuser, claiming to anyone who would listen that I had deserted our home while he was away and that he had no idea where I was. In reality, he knew exactly where I was staying—with family during my training. Despite this, he called my relatives to express that he had no intention of looking for me and didn't care if I came back.

Tunde Oyeneyin, a popular fitness star and founder of the empowerment organization *SPEAK*, discusses profound personal transformation in her book, *Speak - Find Your Voice, Trust Your Gut, and Get from Where You Are to Where You Want to Be.* She writes, *"No matter who we are, no matter where we are, no matter what we are going through or whether we've asked for it, we all have that one moment. A moment when you see clearly how your life might change – the only decision you have to make is if you're going to pay attention to the fact that it's there."*

For me, that pivotal moment came with my husband's phone call to my family. In that instant, I realized he had no intention of changing. I could see clearly how my life would transform if I chose not to return. I envisioned a future filled with freedom and possibility, brighter than I had ever imagined. My decision was final: I seized the opportunity and chose not to go back.

My husband frequently tells anyone who will listen that he wants me back. This statement is both absurd and laughable. A man who genuinely desires his wife's return would actively seek her out and win her over again. Unfortunately, my husband views me as a runaway slave who simply needs to be returned to him. He sought the assistance of church leaders to persuade me to come back, but I was resolute in my decision not to return. Instead of seeking a resolution, he chose to launch a smear campaign against me, portraying himself as the victim. I often wonder which is the bigger *joke: him* or his self-victimization.

In the first two weeks after leaving, my life was reduced to going to work and returning home. I struggled to sleep, often lying awake, crying and questioning how I had tolerated such poor treatment for so long. My appetite vanished, and even the most well-cooked meals tasted bland. During this time, I reflected on my situation and realized that I was free from years of harshness, disrespect, and criticism. This was my chance to reclaim my life and truly live again. I understood that there was no turning back; I needed to take control of my life and steer it in a new direction. I was on the brink of a new chapter, fully aware of the significance of this moment. The deliverance I had prayed for had finally arrived. Although it was a tough decision, stepping through this open door represented my freedom. Indeed, I embraced this opportunity for escape and began my journey into a new life without my husband. To God be the glory.

Chapter Fifteen

THE HEALING BEGINS

"My ability to heal cannot depend on anyone's choices but my own."

- LYSA TERKEURST

John 8:36 states, *"Therefore if the Son makes you free, you shall be free indeed."* I am grateful that Jesus has set me free. In John 10:10, we learn that Jesus came so we could have an abundant life, which is part of what it means to be free. However, it's important to distinguish between *freedom* and *healing*. *Freedom* refers to the state of being free from coercion or constraint. It signifies liberation from confinement, slavery, or the control of another. I found a way out of a marriage that felt like glorified slavery, and I walked through that door into *freedom*.

Conversely, *healing* is the process of restoring health and well-being, making one whole again. At the moment of my freedom, I was still a damaged person, a mere shadow of my true self. My name, *Wura*, means gold, but at that time, I did not represent that name proudly. Just as tarnished gold shows signs of corrosion and discoloration, I too was tarnished. I needed restoration.

Restoration required me to undergo a healing process, which, as expected, took time. After separating from my husband, days turned into weeks, and weeks stretched into months. I persevered, facing each day as it came. Initially, I indulged in self-pity, and God allowed me to grieve as needed. Eventually, He told me it was time to rise from despair and move forward. He provided specific guidance for my healing and encouraged me to exchange the ashes I had been carrying for His beauty. He wanted to rebuild the ruins of my life, but I needed to cooperate with Him. I discovered His intentions for me in Isaiah 61:1-7, and my only responsibility was to work in harmony with His Spirit.

"The Spirit of the Lord God is upon Me, for the Lord has anointed Me to preach good news to the poor. He has sent Me to heal the brokenhearted, to proclaim liberty to the captives, and to open the prison doors for those who are bound. I am here to declare the acceptable year of the Lord and the day of vengeance of our God, to comfort all who mourn, to console those who grieve in Zion, and to provide for them beauty instead of ashes, the oil of joy instead of

mourning, and a garment of praise instead of a spirit of heaviness. They will be called oaks of righteousness, the planting of the Lord for His glory. They will rebuild the ancient ruins, restore the former desolations, and repair the ruined cities, the desolations of many generations. Strangers will stand and feed your flocks, and the sons of foreigners will be your plowmen and vinedressers. But you will be called the priests of the Lord; they will refer to you as the servants of our God. You will enjoy the riches of the Gentiles and boast in their glory. Instead of your shame, you will receive double honor, and instead of confusion, you will rejoice in your portion. In their land, you will possess double; everlasting joy will be yours." (Isaiah 61:1-7)

I found great reassurance in God's promise to give me beauty for ashes. However, I realized that to receive His beauty, I first needed to surrender my ashes to Him. This substitution plan is clear: I give Him my burdens, and in return, He bestows His beauty upon me. This is my message to fellow travelers on the road to redemption from the clutches of the narcissist: as soon as you enter your freedom, let go of your ashes. Hand them over to God so that He can replace them with His beauty.

When it was time to move forward, the first instruction God gave me was to take time to listen to and worship with Minister Dunsin Oyekan, a Nigerian music minister who genuinely seeks the heart of the Father and worships with intention. At first, I didn't understand why God chose Minister Dunsin, but having been a Christian long enough, I knew that if God commends someone to you, there is a divine investment in that person that you need to embrace. As I followed God's servant on social media, I began to understand why God chose him, although it is not my place to share those insights.

Initially, I listened to his music only sporadically. However, one weekend, about four months after separating from my husband, I locked myself in my room, praying and weeping while listening to his songs. The track *"Leave me at the altar with my Father"* captivated my heart that morning, and I found myself listening to it nearly all day. I remained in God's presence until the burden in my heart was lifted, marking the beginning of my healing. A subsequent visit to the doctor confirmed this progress; my test results showed significant improvement, and I knew without a doubt that God was at work in my healing. I felt an overwhelming sense of joy, as healing was something I had prayed for over the years but had been unable to attain due to my environment. Now, I was finally seeing glimpses of a rainbow after the rain.

It has been more than two years since I left my toxic marriage, and while the journey has not been easy, each day has been better than the last. I am walking down what I call *"Recovery Road,"* and I can finally breathe again. I am no longer walking on eggshells, and after years of sleep deprivation, I now sleep well. I committed to therapy, which has helped me release some of the pain and trauma I had stored in my body. Since my separation, my husband has been relentless in his smear campaign, but rather than respond, I have focused on my healing journey. Despite the enormous challenges, I have paid little attention to what others think or say about me. At the beginning of my separation, I tried to defend myself when friends called, but God instructed me to stop and concentrate on my health and healing, assuring me that in due time, He would give me permission to speak.

One year after I fled for my life, God prompted me to share my story with specific individuals. He also allowed me to capture my experiences in the book you now hold. Two years post-escape, I began to share parts of my journey on social media. Being alive to tell my story is something I prayed for, and I am grateful to be here to share it. While much more happened that can't be fully captured in this book, it is enough to know that *El-Roi*, the God who sees all, witnessed everything. Many have judged me without hearing my side, and some have even spoken harshly, especially since my separation from my husband. However, God instructed me to forgive them without reservation. It was challenging, but I chose to do it for my peace with God.

The good news is that my experiences do not define me or reflect who I am. I did not endure this because I am a bad person; rather, my husband chose a path outside the *Will* and *Word* of God. Romans 1:30 states that when people do not retain God in their knowledge, He allows them to become depraved in their thinking. I believe this lack of God leads many within the church to act contrary to His Word. I pray that these individuals will fully return to Jesus and embrace His truth, which, according to John 17:17, is His Word.

Throughout my healing journey, I first had to learn to forgive and love myself again. A fellow survivor of narcissistic abuse, whom I will call Raquel, assured me that God would heal me and bring valuable people into my life. Indeed, those people have entered my life during this season of healing, and I am grateful for them. I have undergone therapy four times, and I appreciate those who understand narcissistic abuse and empathize with victims and survivors. Each of them helped me recognize that none of what I endured was my fault; I was merely a victim of unforeseen circumstances. My *jubilee* has arrived, accompanied by God's promise that I would laugh again. In this *Season of Jubilee*, God has brought people into my life who have made me laugh, and for that, I can only say, *"Thank you, Lord."*

After I forgave myself, God impressed upon me that if I wanted total peace with Him and within myself, my next assignment was to forgive my husband. This was incredibly challenging, and I struggled to understand how I could forgive all the maltreatment I had endured. Yet, Marianne Williamson's quote about unforgiveness kept resurfacing in my *mind: "Unforgiveness is like drinking poison and waiting for the other person to die."* I began to wonder why I would choose to drink poison when I could simply forgive him. It became clear to me that forgiving my husband was imperative.

The Lord reminded me of the parable of the unforgiving servant in Matthew 18:21-35. I also recalled Bishop T.D. Jakes' sermon on unforgiveness, where he declared, *"You have to let it go,"* and I knew I had to. During my research, I encountered warnings about becoming like the abuser due to one's pain, and I had no intention of following that path. In her book, *Forgiving What You Can't Forget*, Lysa Terkeurst writes, *"The more our pain consumes us, the more it will control* us." I realized I needed to let go of the pain and not allow it to dictate my life. I remembered Raquel, my survivor friend, saying that many survivors of abuse risk spiritual destruction if they continue in bitterness instead of forgiving their abuser. Since I did not want to go down that road, everything pointed to the necessity of forgiving my husband.

It was evident to me that God was asking me to give my husband what he had not given *me: love* and forgiveness. However, forgiving the pain of so many years was not easy. Still, forgiveness was a call from God to rise above and emulate His magnanimity. He demonstrated this through Christ, and He expects us to extend the same grace to others. Once I agreed to take that next step, God guided me through what I now call *"Forgiveness* Alley," helping me to release my husband. Forgiveness is not an easy task, but it was essential to prevent the devil from holding me captive through bitterness and unforgiveness.

For anyone living with an abuser, the desire for revenge can be strong. However, whether you choose to stay or leave, it is essential to first forgive yourself and then forgive your abuser in order to heal and move forward with your life. Holding onto bitterness will only hinder your freedom; forgiveness is key. I recently met a woman with the words tattooed on her *arm: "It has to hurt if it is to heal."* Those words resonated deeply with me, prompting a conversation about their significance. Just as a doctor inflicts pain to properly dress a wound, the healing process often involves discomfort. We both concluded that pain is an integral part of healing, and despite how much it hurts, embracing the process is necessary for recovery.

The scriptures recount Joseph's hardships, but ultimately, his suffering served to save his brothers. I believe that, like Joseph, I had to endure profound abuse so that I could help others. With God's grace, I am determined to assist and support women escaping harrowing experiences that can jeopardize mental health. I want to make it clear that I am not a savior, but I draw inspiration from my Master, who chose to share in our suffering to save us. If it were not for the Lord standing by my side, I might not be here to share my story. This drives my desire to help others, with God's assistance.

I am Wura, and I have faced the trials of marital dysfunction and narcissistic abuse. Just as gold must be purified by fire to become its true form, my struggles did not destroy me; instead, they refined me and made me a better person. Now that I am free and purified, I no longer feel ashamed of my past, nor do I hesitate to share my story. I hope that by doing so, I can aid another woman in similar circumstances. Ultimately, however, it is God who will determine the purpose of my story.

As I conclude this chapter, I would like to share some enlightening insights I discovered during my research on the *name Wura.* These insights encapsulate my essence and highlight what makes me unique. They also reflect a special dispensation of grace from the Lord and a significant favor in my life. Perhaps this explains why

He chose to deliver me from the lion's den. To Him be all the glory. Amen.

W	Names starting with 'W' indicate individuals with exceptional business skills who are highly intuitive in their decision-making.
U	The letter 'U' signifies uniqueness, distinguishing individuals from the crowd and highlighting what makes them special.
R	The letter 'R' suggests a strong reliance on emotions, as these individuals are comfortable expressing their feelings and vulnerabilities.
A	The letter 'A' resonates with the energy of the number 1 in Numerology, symbolizing independence and aligning with influential individuals.

Chapter Sixteen

EMPOWERING THE SURVIVOR

"When a toxic person can no longer control you, they will try to control how others see you. The misinformation will feel unfair, but stay above it, trusting that other people will eventually see the truth just like you did."

- JILL BLAKEWAY

I have shared my story, but many women, for various reasons, may never have the chance or privilege to tell theirs. Throughout my research and healing journey, I have encountered numerous women silently crying out for help. Tragically, many abuse victims and survivors sit among us in church, appearing to pray and sing with plastic smiles while suffering internally. Abuse has insidiously infiltrated the church, as it focuses on minor issues. I have lost count of the abuse survivors I have met, and despite their substantial numbers, they represent only a small fraction of the vast ocean of spousal abuse. This chapter is dedicated to these women, aiming to help you understand how to support an abuse survivor when you encounter one.

Any woman who escapes an abuser needs immense love and compassion, particularly because she has endured a relationship with someone who showed no empathy and inflicted repeated wounds. These women are deeply traumatized and require your support, not criticism. They need understanding, not judgment. It is vital to help them recognize that they are not to blame for their experiences, but you must first acknowledge their pain and suffering, regardless of the length of their relationship with the narcissist.

In her article, *"How You Can Help Victims of Narcissistic Abuse,"* Cynthia Bailey-Rug, a childhood victim of narcissistic abuse, *writes, "survivors do not receive a great deal of understanding and support."* However, I believe that *you* can make a difference in the life of a survivor. Living with an abuser is a nightmare, and survivors may initially think they are trapped in a dream from which they will soon awaken. Only the survivor can share their own story, and even fellow survivors can only recount someone else's experience, as each person's journey is unique. Survivors exist in two worlds: the one visible to others and the hidden reality they endure. Although they may feel confused at first, clarity will come with time, and they will realize that nothing that happened was their fault.

Some members of the Christian community have asked me why, if I have forgiven my husband, I have not returned to him or sought reconciliation. My response is that forgiving someone does not imply reconciliation, and sin has consequences. For instance, when Adam and Eve sinned in the Garden of Eden, they were expelled, and boundaries were established to prevent their return. Moreover, God no longer walked with them in the Garden. I urge you, especially *you*, the Christian woman enduring abuse, to reflect on this, particularly when you are told to forgive, forget, and return to your abuser. The mindset of an abuser does not allow for genuine change; experts recommend distancing yourself to avoid further trauma.

Survivors need time to heal, and for true healing and triumph, they must not return to the toxic situations from which they have escaped. If the abuser claims to be a Christian, survivors are often told that the issue is demonic. However, the truth is that abusers are fully aware of their actions; otherwise, they wouldn't hide their behavior from others. A genuinely demonized person would not have the capacity to control their actions in public or only misbehave at home. Therefore, the notion of demonic influence is, in my experience, simply not credible.

Allow me to share insights from my experience and that of others who have escaped their abusers on how you can support survivors of abuse. Survivors are often fragile and on the brink of breaking, but your support can help them heal from their trauma. While you may not have all the answers, your presence can make a significant difference. Here are some tips for supporting survivors effectively:

- First, educate yourself about abuse, especially if you are a pastor or church leader. A list of helpful resources can be found at the end of this book.
- Understand that while survivors are aware of their reality, they often struggle to comprehend how they failed to see through the façade and manipulation they endured for so long.
- Recognize that survivors grieve the loss of wasted years and shattered dreams. It's crucial to allow them to grieve without slipping into depression, as this transition can be very difficult for them.
- Acknowledge the hardships they have faced and treat them with respect and compassion. They need a great deal of tender loving care.

- Avoid dismissing their experiences by saying you don't believe them because their abuser is perceived as a good person. The truth lies with the survivor and possibly their children.

- Many survivors deal with anxiety; encourage them to seek therapy, even if it's just talk therapy, as it can facilitate faster healing.

- Do not suggest restoring the relationship between the survivor and their abuser. This notion can trigger PTSD in survivors.

- Listen attentively. Allow them to express themselves without rushing to end the conversation, even if they repeat themselves. This process is cathartic, and they need your empathetic ear.

- Remind them of their worth. Survivors often feel like nothing more than a glorified servant, sex object, or property to their abuser. Help boost their self-esteem.

- Express your sorrow for the trauma they have endured. Their abuser is unlikely to apologize, and while they may not expect an apology, hearing it from someone who cares can alleviate some of their pain.

- Stay connected and check in on them regularly. Being alone can be overwhelming, and they may feel the urge to self-isolate, which can be harmful.
- Allow them to cry and refrain from blaming them for staying with their abuser. They likely already blame themselves, so don't add to their suffering.
- Do not ask why they stayed. They lived with the narcissist, hoping for change, fueled by love-bombing and occasional gestures of affection that kept their hope alive.
- Do not tell them they should have left; they already know that. The decision to stay is more complicated than it appears, and they had many reasons for doing so.
- Avoid suggesting what they could have done differently. They are painfully aware of those possibilities, and hearing them again only deepens their hurt.
- They are not crazy; even if they feel close to that edge, they are aware of their reality. They need you to acknowledge their experiences and the truth of what happened.

- What a victim of abuse truly needs is understanding, kindness, support, empathy, and non-judgment. Assure them that you recognize their pain and that they are not to blame.
- The survivor must know that God is a God of justice. He cares about what has happened to His child, feels her pain, and offers comfort with His attentive presence.
- Safety is crucial. Ensure they are protected and have a support system that will look out for them, especially since the narcissist may seek revenge.
- Avoid being a liaison between them and their abuser. They need someone they can trust completely; any hint that you are in contact with their abuser may drive them away.
- Encourage them to prioritize sleep, rest, and nutritious meals to help regulate a nervous system that has been traumatized.
- Suggest they see a doctor and consider taking vitamins to boost their energy and improve their health.
- Pray with them regularly, and if they are not connected to a Bible-believing church, encourage them to join one and find a supportive community.

- As they begin to heal, motivate them to engage in activities that bring joy, allowing them to rediscover happiness and rebuild their lives one day at a time.
- The greatest need for a broken and bruised survivor of any form of abuse is validation and empathy, which can significantly speed up their healing process. It is remarkable how they thrive once they move beyond the grieving stage, and the best support we can provide is to accompany them on their journey to recovery.

EPILOGUE

What the Future Holds

During my research into abuse, I discovered that I belong to a group known as *empaths,* characterized by deep compassion for others. Unfortunately, this very compassion often attracts abusers and makes empaths vulnerable to being crushed. The silver lining in my experience is that, despite the trauma I've endured, I have not lost my love or compassion for people.

A few years ago, I founded *"The Empowered Woman Ministry"* to inspire women around the world to fulfill their destinies. In addition to hosting *The Empowered Woman Channel* on YouTube, I have organized women's conferences aimed at encouraging Christian women to strengthen their focus on the Lord.

I have long dreamed of establishing a refuge for abused and struggling women. While I have shared this dream with close friends, I believe it is time to make it a reality. Although I am uncertain how God will bring this vision to fruition, I am committed to taking it one day at a time and watching how it unfolds. The enemy has relentlessly pursued women since the dawn of creation, but we can support one another and overcome this challenge together.

I have dedicated myself to sharing messages of hope on my YouTube channel, and I have come to realize that my purpose is to help liberate other women. I will continue this mission through *"The Empowered Woman Ministry."* While I have additional plans for the future, my primary focus is to empower women and, by God's grace, support those in dire need of liberation from domestic oppression, spousal abuse, and intimate partner violence.

A question that weighs heavily on my mind is, *"Why did God allow all the trauma I experienced?"* Genesis 50:20 offers an answer: it is to save many lives. I invite you to join me on this journey to save *our Sisters* from the enemy's grasp through *NoMA.*

NoMA stands for *No More Abuse,* and it will serve as our means to rescue our sisters from the enemy's vicious hold. We trust the Lord for guidance in carrying out this mission and appreciate your prayers as we embark on this journey.

I want to conclude this book with a *letter of exhortation* to the women still suffering from spousal abuse and to those who have escaped abusive partners.

Dear friend,

I want to begin by expressing my sorrow for the pain and trauma you have endured. It was never God's intention for you to suffer. While my story may differ from yours, I believe there are similarities. This journey has undoubtedly been challenging, and you have likely faced misunderstanding from those who misguidedly supported your abuser. You have shed countless tears and kept many feelings locked away. Please know that *El Roi* has seen everything, and He does not condemn you. He loves you and disapproves of the way you were treated. If you have welcomed Him into your heart, He is your Father, and soon, He will exchange your ashes for beauty. Psalms 124:8 tells us that our help is in the name of the Lord, so do not lose hope; your Redeemer is close and will deliver you miraculously, just as He did for me.

Regardless of your circumstances, hold on to God and maintain your faith. I know you fought valiantly to save your marriage, but now it is time to fight for your future.

You must forgive yourself and your abuser to begin the healing process. Forgiveness is the first step on your path to recovery, and I assure you that healing will come. Even if it seems distant now, trust that it will arrive, and if it takes time, be patient. Morgan Richard Olivier said, "Healing is taking your power back and using it to move forward." Reclaim your power and move ahead, so you can forget the shame of the past and find joy again, for God is poised to do something new in your life.

You are a strong woman, which is why your abuser targeted you, even if you didn't realize it. Reflect on your past accomplishments and believe that you can achieve them again. Yes, *you can!* As I close this letter, remember that you are not alone. God is with you on this journey. As a woman empowered by God to help others, I assure you that He will also empower you to accomplish great things in the next chapter of your life, making all things beautiful again.

I understand that, like me, you may feel compelled to explore the personality traits of your abuser. To assist you, I have compiled a list of resources for further research, should you be interested:

REFERENCES

- The Emotionally Destructive Marriage by Leslie Vernick

- What is Domestic Abuse? - https://www.un.org/en/coronavirus/what-is-domestic-abuse

- Narcissists Who Act Like Christians Part II - https://www.michellehollomon.com/

- The Long-term Effects of Narcissistic Abuse - https://www.charliehealth.com/post/the-long-term-effects-of-narcissistic-abuse

- Impact of Intimate Partner Violence on Women's Mental Health - https://www.ncbi.nlm.nih.gov/pmc/articles/PMC4193378/

LAST WORD

Finally, I want to share the comforting words of Isaiah 54:11-14, which I hope inspire hope for a glorious future:

"O thou afflicted, tossed with tempest, and not comforted, behold, I will lay thy stones with fair colours, and lay thy foundations with sapphires. And I will make thy windows of agates, and thy gates of carbuncles, and all thy borders of pleasant stones. And all thy children shall be taught of the Lord; and great shall be the peace of thy children. In righteousness shalt thou be established: thou shalt be far from oppression; for thou shalt not fear: and from terror; for it shall not come near thee."

I love you, my friend, and I know it won't be long before you are free to live again.

Sincerely,

DL

(Wura, The Empowered Woman)

Houston, Texas

United States of America

December 2025

www.ingramcontent.com/pod-product-compliance
Lightning Source LLC
LaVergne TN
LVHW031925090826
845145LV00018B/2869

* 9 7 8 1 9 6 5 5 9 3 7 7 6 *